I'm Talented . . . Now What?

I'm Talented . . . Now What?

A 16-Week
Workbook for Performing Artists

Michelle Loucadoux

Lanham • Boulder • New York • London

Published by Limelight Editions
An imprint of The Rowman & Littlefield Publishing Group, Inc.
4501 Forbes Boulevard, Suite 200, Lanham, Maryland 20706
www.rowman.com

6 Tinworth Street, London SE11 5AL, United Kingdom

British Library Cataloguing in Publication Information Available

Library of Congress Cataloging-in-Publication Data Available

ISBN 9781538139868 (paper : alk. paper)
ISBN 9781538139875 (electronic)

♾™ The paper used in this publication meets the minimum requirements of
American National Standard for Information Sciences—Permanence of Paper
for Printed Library Materials, ANSI/NISO Z39.48-1992.

Printed in the United States of America

To
Carter Patrick Fraser

May you chase your dreams with joyous abandon.

Contents

Acknowledgments

I don't know how they did it. I was difficult, sensitive, recklessly fearless, and stubborn. I was an outcast, I was obsessive, and I was often grossly ungrateful. But, in their eyes, I was special, beautiful, passionate, and talented, and they did every single little thing they could do to support and encourage my interests. Kay and Dan Lookadoo, you are and have been the most patient and loving parents through every success, every failure, and everything in between, and I am forever grateful.

Thank you to my incredibly passionate literary manager and book agent, Michelle Zeitlin, for your encouragement, your wise advice, and your unending tenacity. Thank you also to the embodiment of class, Shelli Margheritis, whom I am proud to call both my talent agent and my friend.

I would like to thank my tribe of friends, my confidantes, and the sources of my support and inspiration: My "LA Girls"—Kate, Penny, Jenn, Stacey, Kimberly, Kelly, Adrienne, and Melody. I am proud to consider you the friends I call family. Thank you to Matthew—my brother from another mother. This book would not exist without your competitive encouragement. Thank you to the ladies of my "goal groups," who inspire me to overachieve and underachieve with equal voracity: Marissa, Ambika, Christine, Leslie, Zakiya, Crista, Kyra, and Katie.

Thank you to Glenn, for creating the inspiration for this book, and to Bryan, for giving me the respect that made me believe I could write it. And thank you to all of my students, for continuing to inspire me every day.

Lastly, thank you to Patrick. You see everything, and you still love me in spite of and because of it all. You don't want any words, so I won't give you many. I'll just say YDGB™.

Introduction

Choosing to pursue a career in the arts is both brave and noble. It's also sometimes difficult and confusing, because the path to artistic success is rarely logical or linear. Some people randomly decide to show up to audition for *American Idol* and are then catapulted to lifelong fame, while some people who have worked their whole lives to get to Broadway never make it. It's tough out there, but if you're reading this book, you're probably willing to give it a go in hopes that you'll get to do what you love for a living. When you choose to pursue a career in the arts, you are opting in for a life of highs, lows, exhilaration, and rejection. It's a life where there is never a dull moment, and most people who have had long careers in the arts would have had it no other way. The careers of artists are vastly rewarding, the community that is created among artists is unparalleled, and I can assure you that life is never, ever boring. So be encouraged to march forward, courageous and bold artist, into your fantabulous future. This book is here to help you throughout your journey.

Here's the most important thing to know: There are hundreds of things you can do to raise your chances of landing your dream job in the arts. Whether your dream is becoming an Oscar-winning dramatic actor or a hip-hop-dancing YouTube sensation, the best thing you can do for yourself is to learn everything you can about your chosen vocation, plan your path, and prepare for any bumps you might encounter along the way. This book will help you do just that. You'll decide on your dream gigs, do research on the top players in your industry, find a mentor, plan your professional network of connections, find a side hustle, acquire new skills that will help you succeed, discover your personal artistic style, and trick out your social media. You'll also use the book's Coin Calculator to make sure that while you're doing all of these things, you'll still be able to buy groceries. Pursuing your dream job for a living is only fun if it's financially sustainable. (Real talk: you can't be a professional ballet dancer if you can't buy pointe shoes, and you can't become a famous actor if you can't pay for acting lessons.) So let's take some time to explore the ways you can take small steps to achieve your big goals.

First things first: if you've chosen to pick up this workbook, you've spent many hours doing whatever you do best. You've likely spent thousands of hours either singing in a choir, practicing playing guitar, memorizing monologues, or practicing your tango steps. Why? Because you love to do it! Dedication is the name of the game. And to be a successful artist, you have to be dedicated to your craft. If you love what you do, you are inevitably dedicated to pursuing it (if you don't love pursuing your art, you should close this book right now and find something else that you do love to do). Along with dedication, though, comes discipline. If you are dedicated to succeeding in your craft, you must have the discipline to practice it and get better and better at doing it every day. You love what you do, so you do it as much as you can to improve so that you can do it even more. Most dancers spend hours and hours every day in the dance studio and many actors work on a single monologue for months. The better you get at doing what you do, the more you love to do it. The more you love doing what you do, the more you want to practice doing it, and the better you become. Get the idea? Now, that same dedication and discipline you apply to your art . . . should be applied to the *business* of your art as well.

Believe it or not, the business of your art is just as important as the art of your art. If you're interested in being an artist, you're also more than likely going to be a solo entrepreneur. What does that mean? In short, you're going to be in 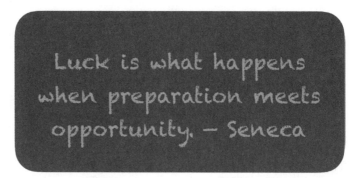 business for yourself. Merriam-Webster defines "entrepreneur" as, "one who organizes, manages, and assumes the risks of a business or enterprise."[1] To be an entrepreneur, you don't have to be the CEO of a Fortune 500 company or walk around in smart suits all day making important, million-dollar business deals in a major metropolitan area. But you *will* be the one who will be organizing, managing, and reaping the rewards (or enduring the failures) of your career as an artist. So welcome to the party, solo entrepreneur. You're officially the president, CEO, CFO, and everything else of Sarah-the-Gospel-Singer, Tom-the-Musical-Theatre-Dancer, or Skylar-the-Indie-Film-Actress Incorporated. (Or not incorporated—that's something for you to talk about with your accountant).

In essence, you are the person in charge of how successful (or unsuccessful) you will be. In this day and age, you do not need to wait for someone to notice you, hire you, and "make you a star." You can take control of your future, create your own jobs, and chart your path to success. Will it always work out exactly according to your plan? Probably not. But if you take actionable steps toward creating your best future, you'll be in a much better place than you were when you started.

Take, for instance, Courtney. Let's say Courtney wants to be a comedic actress. In one scenario, she can move to a big city, start auditioning for as many things as she can, and send out hundreds of headshots to strangers, hoping to get an agent and/or find someone to help her achieve her goal. Anybody heard the phrase "Throwing spaghetti at the wall to see what sticks"? *Or* she could get much more specific. Courtney could decide *exactly* what she wants to act in (let's say it's comedic sitcoms), move to the location where most comedic sitcoms are filmed (Los Angeles), take comedy improv classes, find out who the casting directors are for the show(s) she wants to be on and take a class with them, start writing her own material and work to get it up on YouTube, get a side hustle job at a bar that features stand-up comedy, join a filmmaking group that needs actors to read their screenplays, film her friends on her smartphone as they do snippets of her funny stuff, post those snippets to her social media, volunteer for a charity like Comedy Gives Back, and make a *lot* of professional connections along the way.

Which scenario do you think would be more successful? It's obvious. The more purposeful Courtney is about her goals and her career, the more successful she is likely to be.

"But," you may say, "some people don't have to do all of that work. Some people just easily fall into exactly what they want to do, and they don't have to try at all." Sure, there are those lucky people who are effortlessly successful, but one must then wonder what those people are leaving on the table. How much better could their careers be if they were purposeful about them? This book will challenge you to make the most of your arts career—whether you're effortlessly lucky or not.

This book will also open your mind to more than one career path in your chosen field. Most of today's working artists are freelancers, meaning that they usually piece together multiple jobs (or gigs) to make a career. A few lucky folks will land a long-term job (there is dancer who has been in the New Jersey Ballet for twenty years), but most artists move from job to job. Actors can book a major feature film, work on it for six months, and then they're back to looking for work. A recording artist can drop an album, go on tour, and then need to either get back to creating more music or join the virtual unemployment line. This kind of life can sound scary. (It definitely does to most parents of artists.) But if you take the time to explore ways of working around "working," you will succeed. The exercises in this book will help you discover what you can do while you're waiting to land your dream job and what to do when you're between them as well. If you haven't already been made aware of it, the way you present yourself to the world is another powerful thing to consider to raise your visibility (and thus employability) in your industry. Through the exercises in this book, you'll spend time cultivating your personal artistic style, finding the important people in your field to connect with, learning from a mentor, and creating a social media strat-

> The path from dreams to success does exist. May you have the vision to find it, the courage to get on to it, and the perseverance to follow it.
> — Kalpana Chawla

egy. Every aspect of the way you present yourself and your art should be intentional so that, by the end of this sixteen weeks, you will be well on your way to understanding how to get a successful start in your industry.

In short, this book should open your mind to intentionality in your pursuit of your career. You'll learn how to manifest your future, cultivate new interests, and find new ways to support your artistic endeavors. In short, this book is a big ol' grown-up Mad Lib for you to plan your future. All of the ideas will be your own. And at the end, you'll be more specific, more purposeful, and more inspired to put your art out into the world and to make it a better place.

LET ME TELL YOU A STORY. . . .

Wonder why I chose the colors of the graphics in this book? I'm a *huge* football fan and am super inspired by a quarterback named Russell Wilson. In 2012 Russell Wilson was chosen as a *seventy-fifth* pick to join the National Football League. Everyone told him that he was too short to play football on the national "stage" and overall discounted him as a player. As little as two years later, he led his team, the Seattle Seahawks, to win the Super Bowl, and he remains one of the best quarterbacks in the NFL.

Working a full-time job, taking care of an infant, and finishing my master's degree in business leaves me with not a lot of time to write. All of my friends told me I didn't have time to write a book. But I did write this book—every weekday morning from 4:45 a.m. to 6:15 a.m. So, in honor of the determination of the underrated, I incorporated the colors of the Seattle Seahawks into this book alongside hot pink. Why hot pink? Because I believe it represents my positive and bold essence as an artist.

We are what we repeatedly do. Excellence, then, is not an act but a habit. — Will Durant

HERE'S HOW TO USE THIS BOOK

1. First, set aside a time every day of the week (Monday–Friday) to spend at least twenty to thirty minutes working on your arts career. (You can take the weekends off!) It's imperative that you try to schedule this time at the same time every day and write it into your schedule or calendar. Set an alarm on your phone! Why? Because this happens:

   7 a.m.: "I'm too sleepy. . . . I'll think more clearly later in the day."
   9 a.m.: "Oh no! I'm late for [insert activity here]. I'll do my workbook exercises later."

Noon: "Sure, [insert friend's name here], I'd love to go to lunch and catch up. I can do my exercises tonight."

5 p.m.: "Oh, wow! Thank you. I'd love to take your tickets for tonight to see [insert awesome show here]."

11 p.m.: "I'll start working on my exerc . . . zzzzzz."

If you have a specific time of day at which you are dedicated to doing these exercises, you relieve yourself of the stress of procrastination and you free one little additional corner of your mind for your artistic endeavors.

2. *Repita, por favor.* Many of these exercises are not things that you should only do once. In the interest of time, though, we address a new topic every chapter. For instance, when you research the specifics of jobs in chapter 4, that isn't the only time you should do it. Things change in the arts—sometimes on a daily basis! Likewise, at the end of chapter 10, after you've created your career VIP list, don't just contact those folks once. Keep in touch! You may be the most unique person in the world, but it's very easy for people to forget someone they may have just met once or twice. Remember that this should be *fun.* Or at least it should be interesting. If it's not, you might be in the wrong business.

3. Get creative. You're obviously already creative with your art, but now you should get creative with how you're pursuing it. Don't rule out something because you think it's not exactly the thing you want to do. There is a ballet dancer in the Broadway company of *Phantom of the Opera* who loves to bake. While she was dancing in the show, she decided to create a side hustle of a baking company called The Dancing Baker. (You'll read more about side hustles in chapter 3.) It was so successful that it landed her an appearance on a reality television show called *Sweet Genius*, which then brought about a succession of television acting jobs as a ballerina. The point is that you never know which path you will take to get to your goal, so keep your mind and your options open.

4. *Have fun.* Seriously, life is short. It's not worth it if it's not fun. The world is a huge place, and there are billions of things to do in it. If you're not having fun, you're missing out.

That's it. Easy-peasy, artsy-smartsy. The next page is the first page of the rest of your life. Let's get started.

NOTE

1. *Merriam-Webster.com Dictionary*, s.v. "entrepreneur," accessed September 10, 2019, https://www.merriam-webster.com/dictionary/entrepreneur.

Chapter One

Dream a Little
Dream . . . and a Big One, Too

So you want to be a professional performing artist. Great! You have chosen an exciting and rewarding career! The good thing about the world we live in today is that there are hundreds of ways to make a living in your chosen profession. Whether you're a dancer, an actor, a singer, or an aspiring musical theater performer who does all three, there are countless paths you can take to do those things professionally. The first and most important thing to do is to choose the first path you wish to follow. Note: The *first* path, not the *only* path.

According to LinkedIn, millennials will have an average of four careers in their first ten years out of college.[1] Generation Z is on track to have even more. This is not the 1920s, where you learn to be a cobbler because your father was a cobbler and then you cobble until you die. In today's "gig economy," you can not only choose to have multiple careers but you are generally better off if you do so. Even if you have only three careers in the ten years after college, you could choose to be an actress, a screenwriter, and an editor . . . or a dancer, a choreographer, and a teacher . . . or a director, a cinematographer, and a producer. The list goes on. The more interests and employable skills you have, the more likely you will be to cobble together (see what I did there?) a successful career.

The challenge that faces today's aspiring professionals is not a lack of options. It's having too many options. Do you ever feel like there are just too many things to consider in choosing your future path, so you choose not to choose at all? If you answered in the affirmative, that makes you, well, normal. The question "What do you want to be when you grow up?" is antiquated and can make people feel that they need to choose one definable profession from a list, like choosing a Snickers or a Blow Pop from a bowl of Halloween candy. "I'm a doctor," "I'm an actress," and "I'm a teacher" are no longer labels that are accurate in today's society, for two reasons. The first reason is that these labels no longer accurately define what most members of society are doing for their employment. Now, "I'm a doctor" becomes "I'm a pediatrician and blogger who has just started a nonprofit to connect dogs with sick kids." "I'm an actress" becomes "I'm a film and television actress who creates my own content on YouTube, and I am a personal trainer who gives workout tips to my Airbnb guests."

The second reason why "What do you want to be when you grow up?" is no longer valid is that we humans no longer define ourselves by our occupation. What do you want to be when you grow up? How about kind? Or wise, loving, innovative, or gracious? Now, *those* are good answers to that question. (Also, what is "grown-up," anyway?) The moral of the story is this: *don't worry*. If you make the wrong decision and head down the wrong path, you can always veer off onto a different road, but if you don't decide where you want to go *first*, you'll definitely go nowhere.

For instance, if you want to be a dancer, do you want to go on a world tour dancing with Janet Jackson or do you want to be a corps de ballet dancer in Les Ballets de Monte-Carlo? Or do you want to dance in New York as a Rockette? "I don't care! I'll do anything. I just want to dance!" you might say. That may be true, but the more specific you are about what you want to do, the more likely you are to be successful. *And* the better you can prepare for opportunities that may arise in your not-so-far-off-but-super-exciting future.

In this chapter, you'll spend some time brainstorming which jobs you would love to have—and which jobs you wouldn't. (Sometimes knowing what you don't want is just as helpful as knowing what you *do* want.) You'll also spend time thinking about where you want to live and what kind of lifestyle you'd like to maintain. We won't make any decisions until the end of the week, so write down every idea you might have, good or bad. It may seem silly, but getting your ideas out of the pinball game that is your brain and putting them on the solid ground of a piece of paper is mega-important.

Now, before we start, let's talk a little about how to brainstorm. Storms are not perfect, organized, or pretty, right? In fact, in my experience, they're pretty much chaos. Wind, rain, blowing leaves, and hail? But they're necessary in our planet's ecosystem (and for the hot chocolate industry) to make the pretty stuff grow. So when you're brainstorming, don't be afraid to let it get a little messy. Write down any "bad" ideas

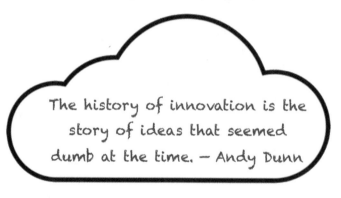

The history of innovation is the story of ideas that seemed dumb at the time. — Andy Dunn

that come to mind. Write down things you think you *never* could do. Get crazy. Think outside the box. Don't judge anything you write. Just write. Try to write down outlandish ideas. Set a timer and *write down every little thing that comes into your brain while your timer is still going.* Why? Crazy ideas open your mind to less crazy but potentially good ideas that you would not normally think of. The only thing you shouldn't do is to write down things you're not passionate about. Passion is everything.

When you're brainstorming, don't be afraid to dream big. And, just as important, don't be afraid to dream small. For instance, the same actor can work as a series regular on a network procedural drama and act in a friend's self-produced YouTube spoof. And both jobs can be just as fulfilling and just as beneficial to her future career. Again, these exercises are just to get your ideas out on paper. Once they're all out in the open, only then can you make an educated decision.

LET ME TELL YOU A STORY. . . .

I have had so many careers in my lifetime that I have stopped counting. I have played principal roles on Broadway, I have worked at Starbucks, I have done quality control for audiobooks, I have danced in ballet companies, I have done stunts in music videos, I have acted in movies, I have been a personal trainer, I have judged dance competitions, I have been a waitress, I have been a blogger, I have been a film producer, I have acted on television shows, I have been an academic dean, I have been a dance teacher, I have choreographed for television shows, I have been a model, I have been a music teacher, I have been a casting director, I have been a college professor, I have directed music videos, and I am now a writer. And this is not a comprehensive list by any stretch of the imagination. You never know where your life is going to go, but the interesting thing is that so much of it connects in interesting ways.

Here is a beautiful example of how so many careers intertwine. A few years ago, I was the chair of the dance department at a college and had the opportunity to speak with the agent who wrote the college's dance curriculum. After chatting for a while, she asked if I'd be interested in teaching ballet at a dance convention. I said yes and then headed out on tour with a few other choreographers/teachers to hopefully inspire young dancers around the globe. On the flight to Omaha, Nebraska, I noticed that one of the choreographers was writing furiously on his laptop. I inquired about what he was writing, and he said he was writing a book. I told him that I had a degree in English and hoped to write a book as well someday. After reading some of my writing, he offered to introduce me to his literary agent. I met his literary agent, we hit it off, and thus this book was born. But the story doesn't stop there. This choreographer was also a director who cast me a year later in a lead role in a movie musical that he was directing. To make a long story short, it's a small world out there, and you never know when one opportunity will lead to a very different next experience.

DAY 1

Set a timer for fifteen to twenty minutes and ask yourself the following question:

What things do I want to accomplish in the next year of my career?

Think big. But also, don't be afraid to think small. (A year can be a pretty short period of time.) But most important, be very specific. Think of what your life outside your career will be like as well. Where and how do you want to live? Here's a little example of an aspiring actor's brainstorm:

Artist: Margot   Specialty: Acting

Take acting class every week for a year.

Write and produce a horror spoof for YouTube.

Be an actor in a haunted house or hayride.

Book a role in an indie horror film.

Live in West Hollywood in a fun apartment.

Get a side gig working at a comic book store.

Host an online horror review show.

Your turn. Go!

DAY 2

Now that we've got the brainstorming juices flowing, let's do an alternative exercise. Let's think of things you *don't* want to do within your career . . . or things you're not great at that you aren't interested in putting the time in to get better at them. For instance, you may want to be a director, but you are not remotely interested in directing television sitcoms. That's a useful piece of information that can absolutely help you narrow your focus. How? Well, if you're not directing sitcoms, maybe you're directing feature films. If your brain recognizes that you don't like one thing, it will automatically search for an alternative solution that you *do* like. So set a timer for ten to twelve minutes and ask yourself:

What things do I not *want to spend my time pursuing in my career?*

This exercise will rule out a lot of options and save you a lot of time and energy if you do it correctly. After you're done with your *don't*s, set another timer for ten to twelve minutes and put a *do* next to each one of your *don't*s. These can be the same as day 1's brainstorm. In fact, if they are, that's great! That means you know exactly what you want to accomplish!

Don't	Do
_____	_____
_____	_____
_____	_____
_____	_____
_____	_____
_____	_____
_____	_____
_____	_____
_____	_____
_____	_____
_____	_____
_____	_____
_____	_____
_____	_____
_____	_____

DAY 3

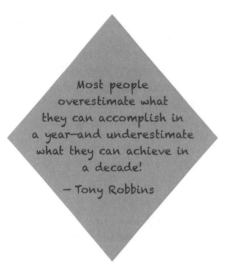

Most people overestimate what they can accomplish in a year—and underestimate what they can achieve in a decade!

— Tony Robbins

Let's continue our trip on the brainstorm train to Successville. It's now time to think about where you would like to be in ten years. If you're eighteen years old, that will be when you're twenty-eight (if that helps to think of it that way). Again, think big *and* think small. Get specific about what your goals are, but consider all parts of your life: career, lifestyle, family, location, and so forth. Set a timer for fifteen to twenty minutes and consider the following:

What do I want to accomplish in my career in the next ten years?

Here's an example:

Artist: Philomena	Specialty: Singer/Songwriter

Drop a complete album of 10 songs all by me.

I want to own my own recording studio.

Have produced a series of music videos.

Buy a car.

I want to have created my own corporation.

Teach local underprivileged kids about music.

Don't be afraid to consider seemingly random ideas. Maybe you want to become a foster parent for puppies, or a marathon runner. Throw that in as well. Hobbies can only make you a happier and more interesting human.

_____

_____

_____

_____

_____

_____

_____

_____

_____

_____

_____

_____

_____

_____

_____

_____

_____

_____

DAY 4

Today is your last day of brainstorming, but it's also the day that's the most fun. Today you're going to ask yourself:

What do I want to accomplish in my career in my lifetime?

I know that sounds like a huge question, but a lot of people don't ask it of themselves—ever. Significantly fewer people ask it of themselves when they're young. This exercise should be both outlandish and inspiring. There are very few things people *can't* achieve if they put their full effort into achieving it, particularly if they have their entire lives to do it. So set a timer and go to work. But first, here's an example:

Artist: Daniel   Specialty: Spoken word

I want to record an album of spoken word.

Collaborate on a song with Avril Lavigne.

Buy and drive a black Mercedes AMG.

Have two kids and a spouse that inspire me.

Tour the world performing my spoken word.

Write a book of poetry.

Perform at Coachella.

Be featured on a talk show.

In my lifetime, I want to . . .

_____

_____

_____

_____

_____

_____

_____

_____

_____

_____

_____

_____

_____

_____

_____

_____

_____

DAY 5

The most difficult thing is the decision to act; the rest is merely tenacity. The fears are paper tigers. You can do anything you decide to do. You can act to change and control your life; and the procedure, the process, is its own reward.
— Amelia Earhart

Now it's time to make some decisions. You've done the brainstorming; now let's choose your favorite ideas. Again, none of this is permanent, so just go with your gut. It's like choosing something from your closet; you have a bunch of clothes you like and have purchased already, so you simply need to choose what to wear today. Read back over your list of future awesome gigs, decide which three you feel most strongly about, and place them below (regardless of whether they're from the one-year or lifetime brainstorming day). After you've chosen your three top goals, do a little soul-searching and decide how important it is to you to achieve these things. Will you absolutely cease to exist if you never get to create a documentary on llamas? Well, give that goal an importance score of 10. Excited about singing the national anthem at a Cubs game, but it's not the most important thing to you? Give that goal a 5. This importance score will help you determine how much of your time you would like to spend on pursuing each of these aims. Here's one example:

Artist: Greg	Specialty: Ballet dancer

Goal	Importance Score (out of 10)
Become a successful ballet dancer	10
Start a blog for male dancers	5
Volunteer at an orphanage to teach dance	8

Now it's your turn:

Goal #1	Importance Score (out of 10)
Goal #2	Importance Score (out of 10)
Goal #3	Importance Score (out of 10)

Choosing three goals in a week seems like a small feat, but a correctly chosen aim, when it is specific and pursued with focus, is rare . . . and highly effective. If, for the next fifteen weeks, you focus on pursuing these three specific goals, you will be surprised at how much you will accomplish.

The last thing you *must* do is schedule the time you plan to work on your future in the arts. Set aside a time (preferably every day) that you do *something* to get you a little closer to your three goals (you'll be more specific about exactly what to do when you've finished this workbook; for now, just do *something*). In the previous example, our aspiring ballet dancer, Greg, can schedule 9 a.m. to 10 a.m. every day to work on his career. From Monday through Wednesday, he can work on his first goal of becoming a great ballet dancer. On Thursdays he can start formatting and setting up his dance blog. Fridays, he can research volunteer opportunities at orphanages. Note that Greg chose to spend more time on the goal that was most important to him. That's great! How you choose to divide your time among your goals is up to you. But it is a choice you should actively make; don't leave it up to chance.

The next thing you should do is put these times in your schedule or planner. Set an alarm on your phone, and keep your appointment with your career as you would an appointment with your future agent. Make a commitment right now to not be a passive participant in your future. Instead, spend a little time every day working to be the creator of your future. Why? What we do consistently adds up. One hour per day on weekdays may not seem like a lot, but over a year, that's 260 hours in *only one year*! That's ten twenty-four-hour days!

LET ME TELL YOU A STORY. . . .

Consistency is key. You must create the *habit* of carving out time to work on cultivating your career in the arts. Habits are formed from repetition. If you do something twice, it does not make a habit. If you keep moving in the correct direction, no matter how slowly you're going, you will eventually get to where you want to be. Remember how this book was written? Consistent 4:45 a.m. to 6:15 a.m. writing sessions. Will you encounter setbacks? Yes! My 4:45 a.m. writing sessions sometimes ended at 5 a.m. with a crying baby. But with consistent commitment to *my* career, this book was done in less than a year. And in a year (or less), you, too, will be well on your way to your most fabulous future.

NOTE

1. Jeffrey R. Young, "How Many Times Will People Change Jobs? The Myth of the Endlessly-Job-Hopping Millennial." EdSurge, February 19, 2019, https://www.edsurge.com/news/2017-07-20-how-many-times-will-people-change-jobs-the-myth-of-the-endlessly-job-hopping-millennial.

Chapter Two

Find Your *Why* and Your *Me*

The things you choose to do in life are very important. In fact, they shape your life experience and how you affect the world around you. But the reason behind *why* you do the things you do is even more important. If you find the right *why* (it's in italics because it's significant) for doing your art, it will both inspire you and keep you wanting to be in the game for longer. Why? Exactly!

When a two-year-old incessantly asks the question, "*Why*?" it's terribly annoying. But it's probably the best question to ask when you're all grown because it gets to the bottom of your motivation, which, in turn, helps you discover if you're on the right path. Here's a great example of a dramatic actress named Cass finding a great *why*:

Q: Why do you want to be an actress?

A: Because I like telling stories.

Q: Why do you like telling stories?

A: Because I think there are people with stories that need to be told.

Q: Why do you want to tell people's stories that need to be told?

A: Because there are a lot of underrepresented groups of people in the world that need to be seen and understood.

Q: Why do you believe there are underrepresented groups of people in the world that need to be seen and understood?

A: Because when I visit my family in Haiti, I see how much they struggle. People don't understand how lucky we are in America and I want to open people's eyes to other parts of the world. I want to play roles in films that change the world's perspective.

Now, *that* is a great reason to act in a film.

Cass's deepest *why* is personal and powerful and has the potential to fuel a lifetime of creating characters. When you find your *why*, you not only find inspiration from somewhere deep in your gut but you also may open your mind to other ways to pursue your *why*. For example, Cass could also pursue photography and create a book of photos showcasing the lives of people in Haiti or start a philanthropic social media campaign. In short, finding your *why* gives you inspiration and options. Your *why* is what fuels your determination.

> Follow your bliss, and the universe will open doors for you where there were only walls.
> — Joseph Campbell

This approach can also be a great thing to explore when doing anything that takes time or energy that you could put elsewhere. For example:

Q: Why am I rearranging my sock drawer?

A: I don't know. I don't really need to do it.

Q: Why am I doing things I don't need to do?

A: Because I'm putting off calling my boss to tell her I can't work tomorrow.

In this case . . . *call your boss*! The truth of the matter is that humans do random things to avoid doing other, meaningful things much more often than they would like to admit. And what's interesting is that your brain will tell you that the inconsequential task is *the most important* thing in the world when it's not at all. *So* . . . if you find yourself actively pursuing useless tasks, check in with yourself and see what the thing is that you probably don't want to do. This takes a very sophisticated level of self-awareness, by the way. Along these lines of thought, it is possible to have a *why* you do your art that isn't serving you. It's also possible that pursuing your art is the equivalent of rearranging your sock drawer. Here's a violinist named Greg who finds a not-so-great *why*:

Q: Why do you want to play with the New York Philharmonic?

A: Because I want to be a top-tier violinist.

Q: Why do you want to be a top-tier violinist?

A: Because that's what I was born to do.

Q: Why do you think that is what you were born to do?

A: Because that's what I've always been told I would do when I grow up. My whole family is in music.

Q: What do you really want to do for a living?

A: I want to be an interior designer.

In this case, Greg has some serious thinking to do. And he's not alone. Many people pursue careers that they aren't passionate about just to gain acceptance from their family, friends, or childhood mentors. Or they decide to pursue a career because it's "easy" or "expected." For instance, "My mom was an artist, and my grandmother was an artist, so . . ." Guess what? Those two facts do not mean that you have to be an artist. If, in going through the exercises in this book, you discover that you don't want to have anything to do with the arts, then you've made a good investment of your time and money. You should work to pursue *your* best future—whatever that may be. Essentially, when you pursue something you're not passionate about, it is the equivalent of rearranging your sock drawer. You're inevitably ignoring what you were put on this planet to do. There is something that everyone is meant to pursue. It takes some people a long time to find their passion, and others know from infancy. If you haven't found it yet, that's totally okay. Your chosen path may be hard or it may not be accepted by your peers and family, but if you find a path that is supported by a strong *why*, you're headed the right way. The best thing you can do is choose boldly and listen to your heart.

After you explore finding your *why*, you'll investigate your *me*. Your *me* is your ideal, best self that you will put out into the world—that is, the kind of artist you want to be. And, guess what? It's influenced largely by your *why*. For instance, do you want to be an ambitious winner-take-all go-getter? Or a compassionate everyone-comes-to-you-for support artist? Sure, we can all be both at times, but it's important to define the underlying essence of your ideal future self, because if you know how you want to present yourself to the world, you'll understand how to market both yourself and your art. *And* you'll know how to best hone your craft to support the kind of artist you want to be.

Your *me* is very related to your *why* because they both define to how you want to relate to the world. Finding your *me* (and your *why*) force you to look deeply inward, make discoveries, and then share the results of those discoveries with the world. It's a multifaceted concept, but if you do it correctly, it's something that will affect your entire future (in your personal and professional life). Here are two dancer/choreographers with very strong and very different ideas of their *me* who have brainstormed words and phrases that describe the type of artist they want to be.

Artist: Tyrone	Specialty: Dancer/choreographer
Edgy	Smart
Innovative	One-of-a-kind
Uncompromising	Perfect
Disruptive	Efficient

Artist: Abby	Specialty: Dancer/choreographer
Good listener	Witty
Whole	Nurturing
Loving	Kind
Environmentally conscious	Gracious

Dancer/choreographers Tyrone and Abby are both great people who will probably have successful futures . . . but very different careers. The type of person you are affects your art, whether you want it to or not. The arts give us the ability to transcend words and convey some sort of higher meaning that connects us as humans. If you're not very specific about the type of *me* you would like to bring to the table through your art, the things you do run the risk of seeming shallow and soulless (which we all know, if you're reading this book, that you aren't).

If you identify the words or phrases that describe the core of your artistic soul, you can use them as the backbone for everything you do. You can also check in on a regular basis to make sure you're still acting or creating in a way that is true to your describing words and, thus, true to yourself. For instance, Tyrone can ask himself, "Is this choreography edgy, innovative, and disruptive?" If not, then he's found a jumping-off point for altering his work . . . or a jumping-off point for redefining himself as an artist. Likewise, if Abby decides that she has not been loving, gracious, and a good listener in her dealings with her fellow dancers, then she has some thinking to do! Defining your *me* is also useful when it comes to decision-making. If you're at an impasse, you can always ask yourself, "Which choice is most congruent with my *me*?" That's generally the best thing to choose.

LET ME TELL YOU A STORY. . . .

Want to know one of my deep and dark secrets? True confession? I eat at work when I'm putting off something I don't want to do. Even when I'm not hungry. No joke. I will legitimately eat the pumpkin ravioli I brought from home at 9:45 a.m. to put off calling someone to have a hard conversation or deliver bad news (which, incidentally, is bad news for *me* around 2 p.m. when I get hungry for the lunch I've already eaten). Interestingly enough, though, I have a sticky note on the top corner of my computer screen where I write my weekly *me* words. This is where I often pause. When I look at the top word—"Disciplined"—away goes the fork and the half-eaten ravioli to finish after I return from the gym.

So let's find your *why* and your *me* so that you can use your art to make the world a better place. Let's get started.

> To be a star, you must shine your own light, follow your own path, and don't worry about darkness, for that is when the stars shine brightest. — Napoleon Hill

DAY 1

Today we're going to start exploring the reasons behind why you want to be an artist. I recommend that you go to three levels of *why* you want to do your art. I have included bonus fourth and fifth levels of *why*, in case you feel that you haven't gotten to the bottom of the deepest part of your motivation. Please take the time to truly reflect in this exercise. It should take some soul-searching, so really explore your *why* from the inner depths of your artist's soul. Your answers can be a sentence or a whole paragraph (or more!). And don't judge your answers. "I want to end hunger" is not a better *why* than "I want to make people laugh." Every *why* is completely valid if it's true.

After you write your first *why*, enter a paraphrased version of your first *why* into the question part of the second *why*.

Why do I want to pursue my art?

_____

_____

_____

_____

_____

_____

Why do I want to _____?

_____

_____

_____

_____

_____

_____

Why do I want to _____?

_____

_____

_____

_____

_____

_____

Why do I want to _____?

_____

_____

_____

_____

_____

_____

Why do I want to _____?

_____

_____

_____

_____

_____

_____

DAY 2

Today you'll be brainstorming your *why* for each of your three chosen dream gigs (see day 5 of week 1). Here's how it works. On the first line, write, "*Why* do I want to [insert job here]?" After you answer the question, take your answer and ask *why* again to the second answer. Then do it again. Again, really spend some time soul-searching and getting real with yourself.

Goal #1

_____

Why do I want to do goal #1?

_____

_____

_____

_____

_____

_____

_____

Why do I want to _____?

_____

_____

_____

_____

_____

_____

_____

Why do I want to _____?

_____

_____

_____

_____

_____

_____

Goal #2

_____

Why do I want to do goal #2?

_____

_____

_____

_____

_____

_____

Why do I want to _____?

_____

_____

_____

_____

_____

_____

Why do I want to _____?

_____

_____

_____

_____

_____

_____

Goal #3

_____

Why do I want to do goal #3?

_____

_____

_____

_____

_____

_____

Why do I want to _____?

_____

_____

_____

_____

Why do I want to _____?

_____

_____

_____

_____

If you happen to have found in this process that some of your three goals' *whys* don't line up with your overall *why*, that's okay. In fact, that's great! That's why we're doing these exercises. Knowledge is power! Perhaps, at this point, you might want to go back to the exercises from week 1 and rethink your three goals with your newly defined *why*. It's always good (in life in general) to check back in with your goals and your trajectory from time to time. Priorities shift and times change. The ability to "pivot" in life is one of the main reasons why many artists are successful.

If one does not know to which port one is sailing,
no wind is favorable. — Seneca

DAY 3

Next, let's find your ideal *me*. You probably already know who you are as a person, but now we want to explore how you will present yourself as you relate to your art. They may be the same, but they also may not. If you're the type of artist who may be asked to embody different characters, explore how you want to be seen in the classroom or rehearsal studio. In the exercise below, brainstorm adjectives for your *me*. Set a timer for ten to fifteen minutes and get creative:

_____   _____

_____   _____

_____   _____

_____   _____

_____   _____

_____   _____

_____   _____

_____   _____

_____   _____

_____   _____

_____   _____

_____   _____

DAY 4

Now you're going to choose your top ten *me* words or phrases, ones that you feel best describe the type of artist you want to be, and put them in order of how strongly you feel about them ("1" being most strongly). These are the words that you will use to shape yourself as an artist and the words you can look back on to make sure that you're staying true to the person you want to be. And don't worry: you can always change your selections. In fact, you should change your words and phrases from time to time to develop different aspects of your personality and to reflect you as you live, learn, and change through time. Ready? Go!

The words or phrases that most strongly represent the *me* that I want to be in the world are:

1. _____

2. _____

3. _____

4. _____

5. _____

6. _____

7. _____

8. _____

9. _____

10. _____

DAY 5

Your last task of the week is to set up your *why*s and your *me*s in places where you will be reminded of them on a daily (or hourly?) basis. Perhaps you will write your main *why* on a piece of poster board and put it directly in your line of sight when you lie in bed. Maybe you will change your e-mail password to be your top three *me* words. Set your phone alarm to wake you up with a label that is one of your *why*s. Write

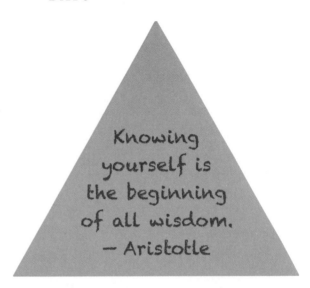

it in your ballet shoes. Make it your screensaver. Write it on the window of your unwashed car. Write it on your bathroom mirror in lipstick and reread it every day while you brush your teeth. *Whatever!*

What we focus on becomes our reality. In an article in *Forbes* magazine, writer Amy Rees Anderson says, "Research has shown that it is our thoughts that drive our emotions, and our emotions that drive our actions. Therefore, if we want to act in a way that will bring us the most success, we have to control our emotions by learning to control our thoughts."[1] And our brains can be pretty forgetful monkeys. So put your *why* and your *me* in as many places as you can. You will want to remember *why* you're working so hard and *who* you are destined to be.

Oh, and *tell people*. Accountability is everything. Often, when you speak your motivation and inspiration out loud, they become even more real. If you tell your friends about why you are pursuing a life in the arts and who you want to be as a person while you do it, they can support you and remind you. And hopefully, you may even inspire them to do the same exercise for themselves.

List three prominent places you will put your main *why*.

1. _____
2. _____
3. _____

List one prominent place each where you
will put your three *why*s that relate to your goals.

1. _____
2. _____
3. _____

List your top three *me* words or phrases.

1. _____

2. _____

3. _____

Now, list three ways you will remind yourself
of your top three *me* words or phrases.

1. _____

2. _____

3. _____

NOTE

1. Amy Rees Anderson, "Never Say Anything about Yourself That You Don't Want to Come True." *Forbes*, January 21, 2015, https://www.forbes.com/sites/amyanderson/2015/01/20/never-say-anything-about-yourself-that-you-dont-want-to-come-true/#6b2d67136f98.

Chapter Three

Burger with a Side of Hustle

While some people go to their first audition or interview and are immediately hired for their dream job, that scenario is pretty rare. *And* there's no guarantee that the dream job is going to last forever. In fact, a lot of jobs in the arts are fairly short-lived. Are you an actress who wants to book the lead in an indie horror film? You'll probably work about one to two months on that horror film. Are you a dancer who wants to perform at the Super Bowl with Janet Jackson? Five days of rehearsal and one day of performing. Then you're back to the exciting world of unemployment. Of course, there are jobs in the arts that can last a very long time (I have a friend who was in *Beauty and the Beast* on Broadway for thirteen years), but those jobs are not the norm. Even if you're a Broadway performer, the average run of an original Broadway musical is only 331 performances.[1] That's around forty-one weeks of work, and that's good! But then, what do you do next?

These statements are not meant to deter you from pursuing a career in the arts. If a career in the arts were not a sustainable possibility, this book would not exist. The fact of the matter is that most artistic jobs are freelance jobs. Freelance workers are self-employed (meaning they work for themselves rather than a company), have a lot of freedom (thus the name), but don't have as much job security as the average employee. Freelancing is a double-edged sword because, while it gives artists the freedom to bounce from fun gig to different fun gig, it also means that there will often be some downtime between gigs.

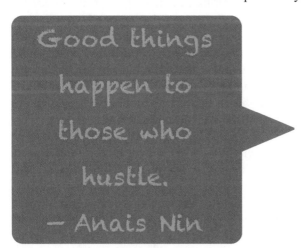

Good things happen to those who hustle.

— Anais Nin

So . . . almost all freelance artists need a side hustle. And successful artistic entrepreneurs are the folks who choose side hustles that they enjoy. There is nothing worse than finishing up a month of brilliant work as the lead actor in a feature film and then having to take a job waiting tables at a local diner to be able to pay your rent. (That is, unless you like serving people, and then it can be great!) Many artists are not willing to entertain thoughts of any vocation that is not their dream job. While that level of focus is admirable, it could get you in some financial trouble in the future. The safest course of action is to plan your side hustle while you are planning and doing your artistic dream gigs. If you have a great side hustle and you set up your contacts for employment in that side hustle ahead of time, there will hopefully be no lapse in your income between artistic jobs.

Here's an example: Sally is a musical theater dancer who has just booked an ensemble role in the cast of the musical *Brigadoon* at Theatre Under the Stars (a great venue in Houston, Texas). Sally packs her bags and heads from New York to Houston for her five-week contract and is thrilled. She has a great time in Houston but realizes that she can't audition for any other shows while she's away (most musical theater auditions take place in New York). She finishes her contract in Texas, heads back to New York, and immediately starts auditioning. After two weeks, she books another dancing ensemble gig in Utah (yay!), but it doesn't start for another month. So, all in all, Sally is unemployed for six weeks between her gigs. Did she save enough money to cover her expenses for that amount of time? Maybe not. (We'll talk about budgeting in a later chapter.) What if it takes her more than two weeks to book another gig? How does she buy groceries and pay for her dance classes if it does?

That's where Sally's side hustle should kick in. If you have a good side hustle and you're cultivating it (and maybe doing it) while you're doing your artistic gigs, you can make sure you're always covering your living costs whether you're working your dream gig or not.

The other important thing to look for in a side hustle (in addition to finding one that you like) is to make sure that it's a job that is flexible. This means that you can choose when you do it or find someone to cover for you if you have a great opportunity in your artistic career. An unnamed actor is well-known for turning down a great audition for a costarring role on a network television show in Los Angeles because he couldn't get away from (and couldn't afford to lose) his demanding "day job." This actor's agent dropped him because he refused this audition, and he hasn't worked since. If you're serious about your arts career, it's imperative that you choose a side hustle that can fit into your artistic pursuits. It's more than likely that, in today's digital age, if you find your side hustle passion, you'll be able to find a way to make money doing it. (Anybody seen the handmade crocheted shark blankets on Etsy lately?)

Just because you may be doing something that is not exactly what you want to do with your big-picture life doesn't mean that it's not important. It also doesn't mean that you should define yourself by your side hustle. The phrase, "I'm just a babysitter," for example, is not something that should ever enter your thought vocabulary. Remember that your side hustle, at this point in your career, is only a means to an end—an important one, but a secondary one. The more appropriate thought would be, "I am babysitting right now to support myself while I write the next great American screenplay because I like to spend time with kids almost as much as I like to spend time writing screenplays." That's artistic focus with a side of practicality.

Additionally, pride can sometimes play a role in deterring artists from seeking out a side hustle. People think that they should be good enough to make a living doing what they've trained to do and that if they pursue a side hustle, they're giving up on their dream. This is not true and is a potentially checkbook-altering misdirection of ego. Cultivating an additional source of income makes you a more diverse and interesting human and is, for all intents and purposes, the opposite of giving up. If you are bristling at the idea of finding alternative sources of income, really do some soul-searching and ask yourself why you're putting up a barrier to your future stability and limiting your freedom to pick and choose future opportunities as they come.

This week, you will take a break from your regularly scheduled, focused work on your arts career and start brainstorming fun and flexible side hustles that can bring in some dough while you're auditioning, taking classes, creating, or performing. Want to be a famous choreographer but love teaching young kids? Are you an aspiring actress with a passion for serving others . . . coffee? Maybe you're a stand-up comedian who happens to be into physical fitness and wants to motivate others to get moving. Maybe you love making jewelry and want to sell it to local boutiques. Whatever your passions, curiosities, or interests, they will likely turn into great side hustles if you cultivate them.

> The dream is free. The hustle is sold separately.
> — Unknown

LET ME TELL YOU A STORY. . . .

While I was a swing on the Broadway production of *Anything Goes*, I worked backstage to get my personal training certification from the National Academy of Sports Medicine. (For those of you who don't know what a swing is, a swing is the person who understudies the ensemble. This sounds like a low-rung sort of gig, but it's a highly specialized skill and one that is super stressful. Well, at least for me it was. I understudied eight ensemble women and two principal roles. That meant I knew every movement of ten different people for the entire 2.5-hour-long show. And yes, I did get them confused from time to time. Long story short: if you meet a swing, you should be impressed, because they're smart and under a lot of pressure.) Once I had my personal training certification, I started training clients in my free time when I wasn't performing (two incomes!). When the show closed a year later, I already had a steady source of dough, and all I had to do was pick up more clients in the interim before I booked my next gig. I have always been very interested in fitness, so working my second job was never a chore. You should always choose a side hustle that makes you happy. Guess what my side hustle is now? Yep. You guessed it. Writing. And I love it. Again, the key is to choose a side hustle that you enjoy doing whether you're already working your dream job or not. You never know: if you're good enough at it, your side hustle could become your second career.

DAY 1

Back to brainstorming. Today, you will brainstorm everything you like to do *outside* of your art. These ideas can be adjacent to your art (e.g., teaching guitar rather than playing it), but they should be different from the things you listed in week 1. Remember that you should never censor yourself when you're brainstorming. Any idea is a good idea. Even the bad ones. Really try to list everything you enjoy doing and go for quantity over quality. You can take the time to go through your answers later. Set a timer for fifteen minutes, and get creative!

_____

_____

_____

_____

_____

_____

_____

_____

_____

_____

_____

_____

DAY 2

First add any other ideas to your list from day 1 that came to mind in the twenty-four hours after you brainstormed. I always do my best brainstorming while I'm not trying to think, so when you do an activity that requires a minimal amount of thinking (sleeping, running, etc.), don't be surprised if great ideas pop into your head after you're done. Now look at your list from day 1, choose your top three favorite activities, and write them below. Under each one of these activities, do a little research and write three ways you can make extra dough doing each one. Here's an example:

Artist: Sandra   Specialty: Performance Artist

I like to take road trips.

1. Sign up to drive Uber or Lyft.

2. Start a travel pictorial blog.

3. Sign up for a website like www.textbroker.com to get paid to write articles on travel.

Note: These are all things Sandra can do on her own time. If she finishes a gig at 4 a.m. after doing her performance art at a charity gala, she can either drive a few folks to where they want to go, upload photos of places she's been, or write an article or two on the subject of travel for a client. Again, flexibility is always the key to a good side hustle. (You also need to make sure that you do—or will—make money doing it. That's the point of a side hustle.)

Now it's your turn. Choose three of your top activities from day 1 and think of ways you could make some extra dough while you do things you like to do. Get creative and think outside the box. And do some research on the possibilities that are out there. You would be surprised at how many different ways there are to make money in our crazy world. Did you know there are pet stylists? Professional mermaids? Lego artists? Professional cuddlers? Snake milkers? If you have an interest, it's more than likely that there's a way to get paid doing something related to it. You just might have to do a little research.

Thing you like to do #1:

_____

Ways to make extra dough doing this:

1. _____

2. _____

3. _____

Thing you like to do #2:

_____

Ways to make extra dough doing this:

1. _____

2. _____

3. _____

Thing you like to do #3:

_____

Ways to make extra dough doing this:

1. _____

2. _____

3. _____

DAY 3

It's research day! Today, you'll choose your top three side hustles from the nine you brainstormed on day 2 and do a little research on them. There are a few things to look out for when you are doing research. First, you should make sure that the source from which you gather your information is reputable and unbiased. Second, you should not take just one source as the last word on any topic; cross-reference what you find with more than one source, and analyze all of the information on a subject (not just what you *want* to find). Your first directive is to find out how much each of the jobs pay. Then, find out if any training, equipment, or preparation is needed to get started. Last, do some research on the flexibility of each of these jobs. Remember: you want maximum money with mega flexibility. Once you have all three of your favorite side hustle details lined up, compare them and choose the most appropriate one for you. If none of your side hustles excites you, then go back to the drawing board. This cannot be stressed enough: *Never* spend your time doing things that don't excite you. And remember:

Maximum Money—Mega Flexibility

Now it's your turn. Crank up your favorite browser and go to town:

Side hustle #1:

_____

Monthly pay:

_____

Training/equipment/prep needed:

_____

Flexibility (on a scale of 1 to 10):

_____

Side hustle #2:

_____

Monthly pay:

_____

Training/equipment/prep needed:

_____

Flexibility (on a scale of 1 to 10):

_____

Side hustle #3:

_____

Monthly pay:

_____

Training/equipment/prep needed:

_____

Flexibility (on a scale of 1 to 10):

_____

DAY 4

Great job! You've officially researched three ways to keep your artistic dreams alive by making sure that you're supporting yourself financially with a side hustle. Now it's time to choose one of the three! Consider the flexibility, the pay, the time (and potentially money) you would need to spend to get that career started, and most of all, take into account your passion for what you would be doing. Once you make your choice, do a little more research and decide on three actionable steps you will take toward turning on the proverbial money hose. And give yourself a time line! For instance, if Sandra the performance artist decides that she

Those at the top of the mountain didn't fall there. — Unknown

wants to drive for Lyft, she should break that side hustle goal down into actionable steps. She might decide that she first should sign up to be a driver by the end of the week, get her car inspected within the next two weeks, and set up a schedule to drive by the end of the month. Voilà! Side hustle initiated. Now, it's your turn:

Side hustle:

_____

Step #1: _____

Time line for Step #1: _____

Step #2: _____

Time line for Step #2: _____

Step #3: _____

Time line for Step #3: _____

DAY 5

For the final day of this week, let's review some of the important and exciting decisions we have made over the past three weeks. You have done a lot of thinking and planning, and, after this chapter, we will be implementing your decisions, so let's sit at the top of this mountain and look down at the path we've climbed before conquering the next peak. First, let's review your three main artistic career goals and your importance scores for each of them. Copy your goals from day 5 of week 1 below:

Goal #1   Importance Score (out of 10)

_____   _____

Goal #2   Importance Score (out of 10)

_____   _____

Goal #3   Importance Score (out of 10)

_____   _____

Now reiterate your main *why* and your top three *me* words below:

Why

_____

_____

_____

_____

_____

_____

Three *Me* Words

1. _____

2. _____

3. _____

And add your chosen side hustle and steps to achieving it here:

Side Hustle

_____

_____

_____

_____

You've made a lot of great decisions in the past few weeks! For the remainder of the workbook, we will be working with these main life decisions as we delve into budgeting, marketing, branding, researching, and overall fabulously creating your own destiny—but with the choices above in mind. (Never lose sight of the prize!)

If at any point in this workbook you feel that your goals or your perspective have shifted, don't worry! Just go back, brainstorm, and choose your new goals, *why*, *me*, and side hustle. Then charge forward into the future!

Finally, take out your phone/planner/wall calendar/personal assistant and *schedule these things*! If you need to sign up for your ESL training class for your side hustle, *put it on your calendar*. If you haven't placed your *why* and *me* reminders in places you will see, *do it*. If you don't have very specific times carved out during your week to work on your artistic goals, *schedule them*. Get the idea? Things that don't get scheduled don't get done. There are billions of distractions in today's world, and the most focused bird gets the chocolate-covered gummy worm. Onward and upward, dear artists.

NOTE

1. Ken Davenport, "Some Startling New Statistics on Broadway Musical Adaptations vs. Original Shows." *The Producer's Perspective* (blog), May 1, 2014, https://www.theproducersperspective.com/my_weblog/2014/05/some-startling-new-statistics-on-broadway-musical-adaptations-vs-original-shows.html.

Chapter Four

The Diva Is in the Details

You now have your dream jobs listed and your side hustle standing by. The goal of this chapter is to help you research the steps to getting your name in lights. One of the most important things you can do in any industry is to learn everything you can learn about an endeavor before beginning it. Have you ever heard the phrase, "Look before you leap"? Well, in this instance, Diva, you should dig in before you dive in, because there are many important things to learn about careers in the arts that are not readily available unless you look. A diva never hurries anyway, so this week, we will be taking our sweet time examining your chosen careers, who currently does them, how you should pursue them, and how much they pay.

This is important, because information you gather in your research of different jobs may eventually influence the decisions you make in your career path. If your dream job is singing backup for a pop star, do you know how you would go about getting that job? Are there open auditions for backup singers? Who is the person in charge of casting backup singers? How much does backup singing pay? Is it a year-round job? Do you have to go on tour? What about your other goals? What about your side hustle?

This week, you will spend some quality time scouring the Internet for *all* information related to your dream jobs and side hustle and hopefully answering questions like the ones above. Research is a huge component of success, and most artists don't do remotely enough of it. And these days, research is *easy*! Back in the old days, you'd have to go to the library and search through dusty boxes of microfiches of old publications (you all probably don't even know what a microfiche is!), but today you just need to crank up your favorite browser and Google away. It cannot be stressed enough: research is *imperative*—for everything.

Most successful corporations have an entire department dedicated to R&D (research and development), into which they put a significant amount of focus and funding. And companies *always* put their time and money where it matters. Did you know that Apple spent 11.6 billion bucks on R&D in 2018? And Amazon? They spent 22.6 billion.[1] That's billion with a *b*. By investing in research, these companies are spending money to become more effective and efficient in the future. They've figured out that money and time spent up front gathering information and figuring out the best way to do things saves a lot of time and money on the back end. Look before you leap. Dig in before you dive in.

Guess what? The same rules apply to careers in the arts. Sadly, very few people in arts careers tend to take time to do the research when they're starting out. But, riddle me this, Batman: Would you rather know more or know less when you go to an audition or an interview for a new gig? Hopefully, you want to know more. For any kind of interview or audition for a new project, you should ask yourself: What kind of projects has the director previously done? What kind of dancers does the choreographer prefer? What kind of pitches does your ideal client prefer? How does the production company you want to work for usually run their tours? That info could come in pretty handy when interviewing or auditioning for a job. Well, ladies and gents, unless you are the most informed person in the world, that kind of info requires a little legwork from your personal research department.

Taking the time to research the projects you're considering will not only help you give a better interview, pitch, or audition but it may also help you decide whether or not to even spend your time on said project (thus saving you more time for studying your craft and pursuing other worthy projects). The more you know, the better off you are. And it's highly likely that at least 75 percent of the aspiring artists who will surround you in auditions, jobs, recording sessions, and so forth have not taken the time to do their research. This fact alone can give you a wonderfully empowering sense of preparedness and confidence even before you walk in the room.

> You have to do the research. If you don't know about something, then you ask the right people who do.
> — Spike Lee

So let's say one of musical theater dancer Donna's dream gigs is to dance in a Broadway show for director and choreographer Susan Stroman. (Good choice: she's an awesome lady who creates some equally awesome shows.) Let's also say that Donna didn't do her research and showed up to a nonunion, open audition for Ms. Stroman's newest show. Let's also say that Donna is 5'1". (Those of you who know "Stro shows" know where we're going with this.) Most of the time, dance auditions for Susan Stroman ask for their auditioning dancers to be taller than 5'5". If you're 5'1" and you walk into an audition full of women who are 5'5" and above, you might be a little caught off guard. Is this to say that Donna shouldn't crash an audition full of supertall women? Not at all. It's Donna's choice whether to attend the audition or not. But she should make sure she's making an *educated* choice before she steps into the room. Again, research is the key.

So how, exactly, do you do your research? Largely, this is up to you and how you choose to work, but there are a few things to keep in mind. First of all, research does not always consist of searching online for information. You can also ask your friends and contacts, you can call one of the artists' unions for information, you can message people on their social with questions, and you can just plain do a few cold calls to organizations. Additionally, sometimes people are more likely to give more detailed intel in person because they can throw in their own opinion without having to put it in writing.

Second, you should consider validating any information you receive. For instance, instead of taking your friend's word that all dancers who do an international tour with a music artist receive a certain salary, you should double-check that with, perhaps, a union or an agent. Ideally, you should find more than one source that gives you the same information. (People may be well intentioned, but they're sometimes wrong.) Lastly, you should always take notes on what you find. Designate a favorite notebook as your "research" notebook and write things down as you find them. You might think that you will remember everything (and you may), but you hopefully will be able to use this notebook for years to come, so write things down so that you can look back and reference them in the future. You might even want to consider a different color pen for each of your goals. The long and the short of it is that the more information you have, the more powerful you are, so let's get to researching.

Schedule time this week to research your dream gigs and your side hustle. This week's exercises are laid out for you, so don't worry about what to research at what time (I will let you know). However, after this week, how much of your time should you spend researching? You have already figured that out! Look back at your importance scores for your main goals from day 5 of chapter 3. Divide the days of the week based on your importance score of these three goals (i.e., if you have scores of 10, 5, and 3, spend three days, one and a half days, and a half day on researching each of these goals). It doesn't have to be exact—just intentional. Set a timer each day for the amount of time you would like to spend learning, and take notes on what you find. For your side hustle research, simply spend time researching when you're waiting. Do research on your smartphone when you're waiting in line at the coffee shop, when you're waiting for the train or bus, when you're waiting for the elevator, and so forth. You'd be surprised how much time we spend waiting in our lives. Now you have something productive to do during that time. In short, you should be continuing to research your industry throughout your career. Even if you set aside ten minutes per day to search for new opportunities or trends, you're likely doing more research than most people.

> Without data, you're just another person with an opinion.
> — W. Edwards Deming

LET ME TELL YOU A STORY. . . .

I was recently contacted by a friend of mine who is a television producer. She was working on creating a new crime show for a large network and asked if I knew of any talented actresses who would be a good host for her new television show. I sent her a few names of women I knew in the industry, and she scheduled auditions for them. (First of all, this is a testament to the fact that who you know in the arts is, perhaps, the most prominent indicator of success. See chapter 10 for more information on setting up your network of contacts.) A few days after the audition, my friend called to let me know that one of the actresses I sent her had booked the job (again, a *very* prestigious job). She raved about how the actress had done research before her audition on the crime that they were highlighting and that she was even able to improvise lines when asked because she was so well versed. She knew the names of investigators, dates, and details that could only have been found with additional research outside the copy. The network executives had been so impressed with this that they said they would be offering this actress the job without even asking her to come in for a callback. Now *that*, my friends, is the power of research. In the midst of a pool of very talented Los Angeles actresses with piles of television credits, the one woman who took the time to do research ended up booking the job.

DAY 1

Today's research topic is *people*. Set a timer and do some research on who is currently successful at doing what you want to be doing. Find at least three people for your goal #1. Do you want to be a voice-over artist for cartoons? Seek out the names of the artists behind your favorite characters and find out as much about them as you can. Want to be a burlesque dancer in Vegas? Check out your favorite venues and discover who is in charge of casting for them. If you can't readily find the information you'd like to know, pick up the phone! Or send an e-mail that says, "I am an aspiring burlesque dancer, and I hope to perform in great shows like yours one day. Would you mind telling me the name of your casting director?" Never underestimate the power of flattery. Dive deep into how the successful people in your industry have become so. What skills do they have? How did they prepare for their careers and subsequent successes? How did they get the job they currently have? Watch YouTube interviews with them, follow them on social media, and, if you're brave, start a conversation with them! (We'll talk about mentors in a later chapter.) Here's an example:

Artist: Mathilda   Specialty: Musical Theatre

Goal #1: Become a swing in a Broadway show
_____

Person who has done it: Jennie Ford
_____
Dance-trained as well as acting and singing
_____
Is very organized: she talked about work ethic a lot
_____
Wrote a series of books on being a swing
_____

Hopefully, your research will cause you to ask other questions and will open up your mind to additional opportunities to learn about your industry. In the previous example, if Mathilda didn't already know about Jennie's books on how to be a swing in a Broadway show, my guess is that she would be intrigued enough to do a little more research and buy and read her books. Or maybe she would be inspired to reach out to Jennie to ask her more questions. The more you research, the more you want to do more research (hopefully). Now, it's your turn. Set your timer and get going. Grab a laptop and notebook, follow your progress, and at the end of your time, enter your top three most intriguing facts below:

Time to spend on research for Goal #1 (don't forget to set a timer!): _____

Goal #1: _____

Person #1 who has done it:_____

Fact #1:

_____

_____

_____

Fact #2:

_____

_____

_____

Fact #3:

_____

_____

_____

Person #2 who has done goal #1:_____

Fact #1:

_____

_____

_____

Fact #2:

_____

_____

_____

Fact #3:

_____

_____

_____

Person #3 who has done goal #1:_____

Fact #1:

_____

_____

_____

Fact #2:

_____

_____

_____

Fact #3:

_____

_____

_____

DAY 2

Today, we will be researching people who have been successful in your other two goals. Chances are, your first goal was the one to which you had delegated the most time, so you should be able to fit the research for your two remaining goals into one day. Don't forget to look at where people who were successful in your art started, where they ended up, and what they needed to do to get where they were going. Look into what skills your people honed, what connections they made, which unions they needed to join, and what side hustles they needed to acquire to succeed. The more you learn about the people who have been successful in your industry, the more you learn about your industry. Set a timer and go!

Honesty and transparency make you vulnerable. Be honest and transparent anyway.
— Mother Teresa

Time to spend on research for Goal #2 (divide your daily allotment of time by 2):

_____

Goal #2: _____

Person #1 who has done it: _____

Fact #1:

_____

_____

_____

Fact #2:

_____

_____

_____

Fact #3:

_____

_____

_____

Person #2 who has done goal #2: _____

Fact #1:

_____

_____

_____

Fact #2:

_____

_____

_____

Fact #3:

_____

_____

_____

Person #3 who has done goal #2: _____

Fact #1:

_____

_____

_____

Fact #2:

_____

_____

_____

Fact #3:

_____

_____

_____

Time to spend on research for Goal #3 (the other half of your time from Goal #2):

_____

Goal #3: _____

Person #1 who has done it: _____

Fact #1:

_____

_____

_____

Fact #2:

_____

_____

_____

Fact #3:

_____

_____

_____

Person #2 who has done goal #3: _____

Fact #1:

_____

_____

_____

Fact #2:

_____

_____

_____

Fact #3:

_____

_____

_____

Person #3 who has done goal #3: _____

Fact #1:

_____

_____

_____

Fact #2:

_____

_____

_____

Fact #3:

_____

_____

_____

Research is creating new knowledge.
— Neil Armstrong

DAY 3

Now that you hopefully know a lot more about success in your art (and you have compiled a great list of potential future mentors), it's time to talk money. This week you will research how much each of your goals pays. I know, I know. You would do it all for free because you love it so much, right? Unfortunately, the world we live in is not free. You have to buy food, pay rent/mortgage, pay for transportation, and you also need to be able to finance some fun! The failure to look at the commerce side of art is one of the largest missteps young artists take. You will eventually put together a list of your expenses and figure out how you will make ends meet in a later chapter, but for today, you'll simply research salaries. This may take some digging, because pay rates are not always readily available. Start with union websites if there are any unions affiliated with your chosen jobs. If not, start reaching out to other people in the industry and ask for a "ballpark" pay scale. Remember that if your chosen goals are not salaried gigs, you should search for the pay rate per gig, day, week, or project. Here are two examples:

Goal #1: Stunt person on a television show

Pay: $ 1,005   **per (amount of time or gig):** Day

Goal #2: Stage combat teacher at a private college

Pay: $ 4,500   **per (amount of time or gig):** Semester

You may find different pay scales for the same job. If so, write them all down, and when you need to use them to calculate, take the mean (or average) of all of the same type of job. Keep in mind that the frequency of your gigs may not be consistent. We will work out how this pay works into your budget in future chapters. For now, just gather data.

Goal #1: _____

Pay: $ _____ per (amount of time or gig): _____

Alternative pay: $ _____ per (amount of time or gig): _____

Goal #2: _____

Pay: $ _____ per (amount of time or gig): _____

Alternative pay: $ _____ per (amount of time or gig): _____

Goal #3: _____

Pay: $ _____ per (amount of time or gig): _____

Alternative pay: $ _____ per (amount of time or gig): _____

DAY 4

Don't forget your side hustle! For your side hustle, it may be a little easier to ask your friends to help you find information rather than researching the headlines. Do you have a friend who is making some extra dough writing a blog, being a nanny, or renting a room in his or her apartment on Airbnb? Chat with your friend and find out what you should do to follow suit. Then do a little online research or make some calls to validate the information you have gathered. Also, if you didn't do it in chapter 3, find out how much dough you will make while performing your side hustle as well.

Person who is successful at your chosen side hustle: _____

Fact #1:

_____

_____

_____

Fact #2:

_____

_____

_____

Fact #3:

_____

_____

_____

Pay: $ _____ per (amount of time or gig): _____

DAY 5

Today is the day to put all of your research to work. You will spend your last day of the week creating action items based on your research. You can pursue these during your weekly time to work on your future goals. Here are some ideas from the examples in this chapter:

Action Item #1
Buy and read Jennie Ford's book on swinging.

Action Item #2
Find and sign up for a stunt class.

Action Item #3
Reach out to person #2 doing goal #1 and ask for specific advice.

Action Item #4
Attend a panel of Broadway swings, take notes, and meet people.

Don't feel as if you have to do all of these things right now. These are just informed ideas of how to move your career ahead, for you to look back at when you have extra time and need extra ideas. Your turn!

Action Item #1

_____

_____

_____

Action Item #2

_____

_____

_____

Action Item #3

_____

_____

_____

Action Item #4

_____

_____

_____

Chapter Four

Action Item #5

_____

_____

_____

NOTE

1. Walter Loeb, "Amazon Is the Biggest Investor in the Future, Spends $22.6 Billion on R&D." *Forbes*, November 6, 2018, https://www.forbes.com/sites/walterloeb/2018/11/01/amazon-is-biggest-investor-for-the-future/#4166e5971f1d.

Chapter Five

The Mentor Mambo

There is no better way to plan for success than to glean wisdom from artists who have already done it. If you've done your research in week 4, you should already know the key players in your chosen field, and now it's time to reach out to them. Wisdom from mentors can give you an important edge in your path to success. Having friends in high places can not only be beneficial to the mentee but mentors also get the benefit of feeling great about passing down their wisdom. Did you know that a *lot* of *very* successful people have mentors?

Our chief want in life is somebody who will make us do what we can.
— Ralph Waldo Emerson

Steve Jobs (the cofounder of Apple and many other things) was the mentor for the founder of Facebook (Mark Zuckerberg),[1] Oprah was Lindsay Lohan's mentor,[2] and before that, Oprah herself was mentored by the late Maya Angelou.[3] Wouldn't we all have liked to have been a fly on the wall in those meetings? Now was Maya Angelou solely responsible for making Oprah the megastar mogul that she is today? Not likely. But I'm guessing she definitely helped provide advice along the way.

First things first, though. What, exactly, *is* a mentor? The short explanation is that a mentor is any person who has already accomplished a version of what you plan to accomplish. Mentors can not only provide advice on how to pursue your goals but also introduce you to other influential people in the industry, give you direction during confusing times, motivate you when times are tough, or even hire you! Most important, a mentor should be your role model for how to act, communicate, and present yourself to your artistic community.

Here's the difficult part: finding a mentor can be a bit tricky. Some folks might not be interested in coaching aspiring artists. And others just might not have the time. One of your challenges in this chapter will be developing the bravery to ask (and sometimes be rejected). Remember, you have to kiss a lot of frogs to find your prince. The path toward finding a mentor can be a little dicey, and learning to ask for what you want can be scary, but I guarantee you will come out braver on the other side. And hopefully, eventually, you will nab a mentor (or two)! (Incidentally, learning to ask for what you want in life is a skill that can translate to a plethora of situations and is something everyone should attempt to acquire.)

A key thing to keep in mind when you contact famous or busy people is that you should *always* respect their time. Be concise and specific in your communication and remember to tell your potential mentor your *why* from chapter 2 (so you can play the "Pizzicato Polka" on their heartstrings). Remember that this person has very limited time, so questions like "How did you get into acting in film?" are not as quickly answered as "What would be the one piece of advice you would give to someone auditioning for a lead role in a romantic comedy?" Specificity is key when asking questions of busy people. Come up with questions that can be answered in a few sentences or less so that they can give you great advice and get out quickly. Additionally, if you have not done your research, and you ask a prospective mentor a question that is easily answered on the Internet, you're more likely to be turned down. Busy people appreciate it when people who approach them have done their research. It not only saves prospective mentors time that would be spent explaining their past but it's also flattering.

There are many ways to approach your accomplished artist. Want to be a dancer on Broadway? Ask a thoughtful question and send it in a direct message on Instagram to an ensemble member in your favorite show. Want to be an indie film actor? Buy a pass to a film festival and bring your list of questions to the Q-and-A sessions at the end of the screenings. Again, your mentor should love paying it forward, so if a prospective mentor seems not so interested, you should look elsewhere. You should also be realistic when choosing your future advice-giver. If you want to be a singer/songwriter, it might not be the best use of your time to reach out to Adele. You're welcome to roll the dice, and you may just luck out and roll a seven on the craps table, but you might also want to have a few more who are not Grammy-winning international superstars in mind.

When you choose who you would like to be your mentor, don't just e-mail a message like, "Hey, my name is Fred. Do you want to be my mentor?" Consider this as you would any potential dating relationship. You wouldn't propose to a complete stranger on your first date (or at least most of you wouldn't), so why would you ask a complete stranger to be your mentor? Develop a relationship first! Reach out with a flattering DM or e-mail, ask a few thoughtful questions, and see if you get a response. If you do, then great! Continue to "date" your mentor until you feel that the time is right to "pop the question." There is no official mentor paperwork or secret handshake when you lock down a mentor, but it's great to have someone officially give you the thumbs-up and show willingness to help you out on a semiregular basis. If this happens, you have more than likely already proven yourself to be a thoughtful, focused, upstanding citizen who will not be overly annoying or high-maintenance.

When and how you communicate with your mentor is imperative to lock down. Much like dancing the mambo, you need to "feel out" your dance partner. The mentor mambo is all about taking into account the subtleties of communication and reading between the lines. If you get a terse response, your mentor or prospective mentor is probably busy, and you should lay off the communication for a while. Similarly, if your mentor or prospective mentor is enthusiastic, feel free to be enthusiastic as well. Here are a few things to keep in mind in this communication:

- Keep up with what your mentor or prospective mentor is doing, and make sure to comment on any recent accomplishments you've heard about when you reach out. (But don't be creepy. "How was your colonoscopy?" and "How much money did you make on that last film?" are obviously inappropriate questions.)
- After your initial encounter, you might want to consider letting your prospective mentor know a little bit about yourself and what you're up to. Any good mentor wants to feel that his or her hard-earned advice will not go to waste.
- Send updates on any advice that is given. Mentors do not like for their hard-earned advice to be sucked into a black hole of noncommunication. If, for instance, your mentor suggests that you sing a particular song at an upcoming audition, let your mentor know how it went the next time you chat.
- Offer added value to their lives! You'd be surprised how far a thank-you card, a crocheted scarf, or an offer of free tickets to your upcoming show/film festival will go. You don't have to wine and dine your mentor, but it would be nice from time to time to show your gratitude in some form other than an e-mail.

Finally, you should keep track of your communication with your mentor. While you may think you'll remember everything you send to your mentor, you also may not. If you keep a little record of the date you communicated, what you said, and any feedback given, you will stave off the risk of asking the same question twice or contacting your mentor too much (or too little!).

The purpose of finding a mentor is to have someone in your corner who has been there and done that. The performing arts are not rocket science, but there is a *lot* to be learned if you're a newbie. Do you have to have a mentor to be successful in the performing arts? No. Does it help your chances of becoming successful if you do? Yes. This book alone will not make you famous, but if you follow the advice in these pages, you are more likely to be successful than if you don't. And why not take *every* opportunity you can to enhance your visibility, your network of artists, and your knowledge of your industry?

Success isn't always about greatness. It's about consistency. Consistent hard work leads to success. Greatness will come. — Dwayne Johnson

LET ME TELL YOU A STORY. . . .

I have mentored many, many young people in my day and I have, at one point or another, gotten them all jobs in the industry. (And a few of them are my go-to baby-sitters.) If I look from an outsider's perspective, I can see that there are a few reasons for this. First, my mentees are usually at the forefront of my mind. In one week, one mentee texted me to ask my advice on a choreographer with whom she had had a falling-out. Another mentee e-mailed me and asked if I had suggestions for a 1960s song that she might sing for a particular appointment with a casting director. A third mentee reached out to see if I might recommend an ENT doctor in the area. I'm always happy to give these folks advice. And as they are present in my mind, when a friend calls asking for recommendations for casting or for new projects to fund or for just an assistant on set, these people are the first people I think of. Additionally, because I have put a good amount of work into these lovely young people's careers, I want to show them off to the world: "Look at these great people I have helped along their ways." Similarly, when I was performing on Broadway in my first original cast, the daughter of one of my mom's friends reached out to me via e-mail, asking some great questions about my career and the industry. I was *so flattered* that I not only responded but also invited her to the theater for a backstage tour. Doing another person a favor actually makes you like the person more. This exact reason is why the mentor model is so successful and rewarding for both the mentor and the mentee.

DAY 1

Today you will be choosing the artists you would like to consider as potential mentors. You can look back at your notes from your research in earlier chapters for ideas, but also take time to brainstorm other potential people who might seem a little outside the box. Say you want to be a television director. Your mentor does not particularly have to be a successful television director but could also be a producer or a network executive. Your mentor also does not necessarily need to be someone who is older than you. If they've been there and done that, age generally doesn't matter. Think past the proscenium and think about who has the skill set or overall wisdom to help you improve.

Set your timer for today's exercise and start compiling ideas. It's okay for now if you don't have all of the information you might need to contact these people. If one of the people you write down in your brainstorming reads something like "that guy with the mohawk who writes all of those creepy plays about decapitation," it's great. And at least you'll definitely know how to search for him tomorrow, when we get to the research section!

_____

_____

_____

_____

_____

_____

_____

_____

_____

_____

_____

_____

_____

_____

_____

_____

_____

DAY 2

Now it's time to do some more research. Today you'll choose your top three potential mentors and find out everything you can about them. How did they get started in their career? Where are they from? Are there any interviews you can find with them? What do their Twitter and Instagram feeds look like? Do they seem like they would be open to starting a conversation with a developing artist? Find the most current information you can dig up. But keep it professional. (Don't be a cyber stalker; that will not be likely to nab you a mentor.) As you research, take notes. Divide your allotted time today into three parts and see how much you can learn about your person in that time.

Mentor Contender #1

_____

Timer set for _____ minutes

Notes:

_____

_____

_____

_____

_____

_____

_____

_____

_____

_____

_____

_____

Mentor Contender #2

_____

Timer set for _____ minutes

Notes:

_____

_____

_____

_____

_____

_____

_____

_____

_____

_____

_____

_____

Mentor Contender #3

_____

Timer set for _____ minutes

Notes:

_____

_____

_____

_____

_____

_____

_____

_____

_____

_____

_____

_____

DAY 3

Today you'll choose your mentor! Well, you'll choose the *first* person you'll *plan* to pursue to *eventually maybe* be a mentor. Remember, the first person you approach may not be interested. Or the person may be interested but may not have the time to help you out. Have you heard the phrase, "It's not about you, it's about me"? Well, that is just as applicable to finding a mentor as it is to dating, so don't get disgruntled if it doesn't work out the first time. Having said that, let's give it a go!

If I have seen further, it is by standing on the shoulders of giants. — Isaac Newton

Look back at your research from yesterday. Which of your three candidates did you relate to the most? Which seems willing to help someone else out? Who seems the most accessible and relatable to your most prominent chosen career path? Which person seems like the type of person you would want to spend time with? You'll be spending at least a little bit of time with your mentor, so if one potential mentor's voice makes your skin crawl, you should probably choose someone else.

You should also remember that this is someone who should be at least kind-of accessible. Your mentor should be a person who is currently climbing the same ladder of success that you're climbing (same industry or career path) but is usually just a few rungs higher than you and not at the very top. If you're a dancer in college who wants to join a ballet company and work your way up through the ranks to eventually be a principal dancer, you might want to consider choosing a dancer in the corps de ballet of your favorite company to reach out to rather than Misty Copeland. You would be surprised how many people forget to climb the rungs of the ladder between starting out and megastardom. Your best bet is to find the person who is the perfect balance between knowledgeable and experienced and free enough to take the time to mentor you.

Quick note: If you are a little unsure of exactly which of your goals from earlier chapters you want to pursue, it doesn't matter. You're keeping your options open, and that is great. Don't feel trapped in one specific career path. You can always go back and change your mind. But you don't know if things will work out if you don't wholeheartedly give it a try.

So let's go for it.

My first-choice mentor is: _____.

Take a break for now, and tomorrow we will reach out and start your mentorship journey.

DAY 4

Now let's choose how you plan to engage with your future mentor. Do you have a mutual friend who might be willing to connect you via e-mail to make an introduction? Who do you know who might know your future mentor? Is there a place you might be able to meet your mentor in person? Does the person you have in mind teach a class somewhere that you might attend or sign autographs at a stage door where you might introduce yourself? The arts industries are usually pretty small worlds once you get into them, so check out your research from earlier this week and ask yourself, Do I know anyone who has worked on any of the jobs that my potential mentor has done?

Do you know anyone in the cities that your mentor has worked in who might know someone who could connect you? Have you played the Kevin Bacon game? Well, play it with yourself and your mentor. A personal connection, even if it's far removed, is always better than a "cold introduction."

If a friend from your improv comedy team reaches out to you to say that her sister's friend's daughter wants to e-mail you because she has been following your career and wants to do multicam comedies like you, you're more likely to do your friend a solid and reply than you are to reply to a random DM on social media. That is not to say that a DM is a bad thing; it just has a lower rate of response. If you can't find someone to introduce you, that's okay, too. You'll just need to lay some groundwork first. First, make sure to follow your person. Second, make sure to engage with the person's posts when appropriate (but again, don't be a creeper). Only then should you reach out and e-introduce yourself.

When you've decided which way you will be reaching out to your mentor, you should then craft your letter. Here's a great sample mentor introduction for a person who does not have an introduction or personal connection to her prospective mentor:

> Hi, Donna! My name is Greta Fisher, and I'm a senior at Florida State University studying acting. I have been watching your car insurance commercials for years and you are absolutely hilarious. It's so cool that you are a recurring character on multiple national network commercials! I am graduating in May, and I am so excited to move to Los Angeles in hopes of being a commercial actress (like you!). I hope to make the world a more joyous place by making as many people laugh as I can. Do you have any recommendations for a place in LA to study acting that would help me get better at commercial auditions? Thank you in advance for your help! I've attached a picture of me and my cat (I love your cat's Instagram as well, by the way!) Take care!

Why is this a great letter? First, Greta introduces herself and identifies herself as an aspiring artist. Then she indicates that she is familiar with Donna's work and expresses admiration for it (without being weirdly gushy). Next, she states the fact that she hopes to enter the same industry and finally (and most importantly) asks a *very* specific easily answerable question. If you don't ask a question, you won't get a response, and you won't incite a conversation. And remember, if it's a broad question that will require more than a paragraph to answer, assume that your potential mentor will not have time to answer it. Then Greta states a brief version of her *why*. Finally, Greta smartly attaches a picture in an attempt to establish a connection between herself and her mentor that is not related to the industry. This makes Greta seem more human, because Donna can see Greta's smiling face, and it hopefully establishes a human connection in addition to the industry connection.

Now it's your turn. If you plan to engage with your mentor in writing, you can draft your letter/message below (remember to keep it short):

_____

_____

_____

_____

_____

_____

_____

_____

_____

_____

_____

_____

_____

_____

_____

_____

_____

DAY 5

Now that you've engaged your mentor, today we will be setting up a log to track your communication with your mentor. I like to call today's entry "how not to be annoying." You're probably not an annoying person in general, but if you e-mail or message your mentor too much, you could be viewed as such. Again, it's like dating. After you e-mail, meet, or message your mentor, *wait*. If you wait a week and don't hear anything back, you can reach out again. If you don't get an answer after a second attempt at contact, it's time to pursue another mentor. And that's *fine*! It's not a personal affront to you; your prospective mentor is probably just busy or doesn't check messages that often. And if the person is too busy to reply to your first message, then he or she would probably not have been a good mentor anyway. Choose another person and start again.

If you do get a message back from your person, that's great! Now you have to use your Spidey sense to gauge whether you should respond or not. Did your person ask you a question in return or just answer your question? If there's a question, you should respond in the next few days. If not, you should wait until you either have some new information to relay or you have another question. After two or three answered questions, I'd recommend an offer of something. Offer tickets to your next show, send a small gift, repost a few of your prospect's promotional posts, or do something else that might add value to the person's life. If your future mentor has spent enough time to answer two or three of your questions, you should find a way to pay the person back. You could even find an article or online resource that pertains to something the possible mentor is interested in. For instance, if your person has a kid in New York, share the Kid on the Town website, which points people to cultural events that are kid-friendly. You don't have to spend a ton of money and wine and dine these folks; you just need to find a creative or useful way to add value to their lives. Here's how you should track your mentor communication below.

Date	Communication	Question/Comment/Offer	Outcome
March 2, 2020	E-mail	Do you recommend I get my Actor's Equity card before moving to New York?	E-mailed back: Don't get it yet. (No Question)
March 25, 2020	E-mail	Do you have a voice teacher you recommend in New York?	No response
April 1, 2020	Comment on Instagram post	I love your new album! Do you have a voice teacher you recommend?	Responded on Instagram
April 18, 2020	E-mail	Offer for free tickets to my off-Broadway musical	Responded: Can't attend but good luck
April 30, 2020	E-mail	Will you be my mentor?	Yes! E-mail me any questions you have

It may seem like a waste of time to be this specific about tracking communication, but sometimes we can lose track of time. Six months could go by in a flash and before you know it, your mentor has forgotten about you or changed contact information. *Or you don't remember that you contacted him or her five times within two weeks, asking the same question.* Either way, if you keep track of communication, you can make sure to be respectful of your mentor's time and thoughtful about how and when you reach out. We will discuss more about networking in later chapters, but in the meantime, keep track of your communication.

Date	Communication	Question/Comment/Offer	Outcome

NOTES

1. Ilan Mochari, "Steve Jobs's Early Advice to Mark Zuckerberg: Go East," *Inc.*, September 29, 2015, https://www.inc.com/ilan-mochari/visit-india-creativity.html.

2. Michelle Darrisaw, "Lindsay Lohan Credits Oprah for Positively Transforming Her Life," *Oprah Magazine*, October 18, 2019, https://www.oprahmag.com/entertainment/tv-movies/a25834367/lindsay-lohan-oprah-beach-club-interview.

3. Lesley Messer, "Oprah Winfrey Remembers Her Mentor Maya Angelou," ABC News, May 28, 2014, https://abcnews.go.com/Entertainment/oprah-winfrey-remembers-mentor-maya-angelou/story?id=23901061.

Chapter Six

Breaking the Fourth Wall of Finances

You've got big dreams. (If you don't, go back to chapter 1.) You also probably have an equally big rent/mortgage/college loan/car payment. Dreaming is good, but not starving tastes better. This chapter will help you determine whether your artistic pursuits are financially sustainable . . . and what to do if they aren't.

This workbook is obviously not about money, but knowing how to deal with your finances is a must in the entertainment industry. You can't go to an audition to sing in a new show in Las Vegas if you can't afford to put gas in your car to get there. If you can't afford to take dance classes, you will eventually lose your strength and your edge. Even if you don't want to think about your finances, you will have to sooner rather than later. I understand that some people feel uncomfortable talking about money. A lot of folks feel that having a lot of money is bad or that "the love of money is the root of all evil" (1 Timothy 6:10, King James Version). You don't have to love money (in fact, I wouldn't recommend it), but I implore you to please work to put all preconceived notions about money aside while working through this chapter, and pay attention. The topic of money can be polarizing, but we're not going to talk about anything in this chapter other than how to pay your current bills and plan for your future bills—well, and we'll take one day to envision your ideal financial future.

In this day and age, there are billions of ways to add some coins to your pocket. Technology has enabled a culture where you can literally make extra money with your phone or computer. You can write articles online for money, you can Airbnb your extra room, you can deliver for Postmates, you can add your profile to a babysitting app, or you can post a notice to social media that you are teaching voice/dance/acting lessons from your home. Would you prefer to be receiving all of your income from your checks from touring with an artist/dancing on Broadway/residuals from your most

> A big part of financial freedom is having your heart and mind free from worry about the what-ifs of life.
> — Suze Orman

recent television show/royalties from your new hit single? Of course you would. Do you also need to pay your bills while you're working toward making these awesome dreams happen? Yep.

The key to keeping your finances above the shark-infested waters of rent collectors and credit card debt is knowing how much it costs for you to live from month to month. If you know what you need, you can make a plan to bring in enough dough to survive by piecing together your gigs in your art, your side hustle, and maybe an additional source of income. First, we will spend some time using the Coin Calculator to determine how much moola you need to pay your bills. Second, you'll determine the difference between what you're currently making and what you need to make (and if you're making more, we will discuss what to do with extra cash). Third, we will create a plan for your future self and your big (and presumably expensive) goals. I cannot stress this enough: Finances do not go away if you ignore them. In fact, they get uglier and meaner with every day that you don't pay attention, particularly if you are living beyond your current means. You *must* know and track how much you are spending and where you are spending it. If you don't track it, it will balloon, and you will be in credit card debt faster than you can say *Beetlejuice the Musical*.

While we are at it, let's take a moment to talk about credit cards. Credit cards are like that really useful but really sharp knife in your drawer that can cut through anything—including your finger. Should you even have a credit card? Yes. You never know when you are going to have an emergency, and you also want to build your (good) credit history. But putting expenses on credit cards, unless you can pay them off within a month, is a very, very bad idea, because you will have to pay interest on your balance, and things can easily snowball into tens of thousands of dollars of debt. Again, this is not a book about finances, so I highly recommend you pick up a book (like *The Thriving Artists*, by Joe Abraham and Christine Negherbon) if you feel you could stand to learn more about how money works (and how to work it).

Incidentally, if you happen to be in a place where you're not paying your own bills, congratulations! Thank your parents/significant other/family member/generous friend. For the exercises on day 1 and other current expense prompts, research and enter what you would be paying in your area if you weren't such a lucky duck. The Zillow app is a good place to find rents, Kelley Blue Book is a good place to find car-payment examples, and so on. If you find how much you might need to pay when/ if you're out on your own, you can make a plan for it. And if you are making cash and don't have to spend it on surviving, put that dough away, because you're likely to encounter a rainy day sooner rather than later.

Finally, remember that art and commerce work together every day. People are thrilled to pay top dollar to see Broadway shows, you are happy to download a friend's new track for $1.29 on iTunes, and Hulu and Netflix are thriving businesses. Why? Humans are excited and completely willing to pay for good art. Do you create good art? Chances are, if you're reading this book, your answer is yes (or it should be). You are *worth* being paid to do what you have inevitably worked *years* to learn how to do. Don't undervalue yourself as an artist. Do not agree to dance, act, sing, or create for free because you don't feel that you or your art are worth money. You are! Sure, people agree to do things for free to earn experience and make connections, and that is absolutely valid. If that is not the case, though, you should consider yourself an up-and-coming professional artist, and you should be compensated accordingly. Please, pretty please, know your worth and the worth of your art, and ask to be compensated for sharing it with the world.

LET ME TELL YOU A STORY. . . .

When I was offered my first Broadway show, *Beauty and the Beast*, and my agent told me how much I would be making, I screamed, cried, called my mother, and quit my job at the restaurant I was working at. A whole $1,381 per week in 2004 wasn't too shabby, and if I went on for the role I was understudying, I would receive *double* that. I was young and excited and, well, as green as Elphaba's backside on a warm day in Oz. After calling everyone I knew to tell them the good news and walking by the Lunt-Fontanne Theatre on Forty-Sixth Street to take the obligatory "I just got my first Broadway show" photo, I called my three buddies, Erin, Kraig Paul, and Tom, and told them I would be treating everyone to a fancy dinner in honor of my newfound success. The four of us gathered at a restaurant on Ninth Avenue; ordered fancy wine, ceviche, and filet mignon (medium rare); and when the bill for four hundred dollars arrived, I put it on a credit card. I cared not, for I was to be the newest princess of Broadway for a long and successful reign.

I was thrilled to perform with such a beautifully talented cast and was doing a kick line on cloud nine as I started rehearsals. Until my first paycheck arrived: $821. Wait . . . what? I was floored. I thought I was going to be rolling in dough, but with my first glance at that check, the hard reality hit me that I would be covering my Midtown Manhattan rent, groceries, and other bills, and that was about it. I wondered what had happened. Well, I know now: my agent and taxes happened. Many young performers forget to factor in taxes and payments to agents and managers when they look at pay rates. And I was one of those folks. While I was still grateful to have a steady job on Broadway, I looked at the receipt for that four-hundred-dollar dinner in my wallet with a new understanding and walked back to my old job at the restaurant to see if they would let me work weekday lunches.

Many of us like to ignore how much life costs and just assume that it will all be okay. One of my favorite mantras in those early days on Broadway was, "I don't make enough money to pay my bills and take all of these lessons, but I'm sure I'll book a commercial this month, so it will be okay." That is *not* the way to approach your finances! Trust me, that approach does not work *at all*. When you don't book that commercial one month, do you know how you will buy your gas and groceries? Credit cards. And the credit card slide is a slippery slope, my friends. I guarantee that if you ignore your finances like I did, it *won't* be okay. But if you stop and shine a spotlight on your finances sooner rather than later, you will be off to a great start. The idea here is to get your finances under control and then not worry about them. If you're worried about how you will pay your phone bill, you are likely not spending as much energy worrying about what to sing for that audition. And that is a disservice to you and your artistry. Let's get this money thing locked down so you can focus on the important stuff.

DAY 1

Pull out your banking app, and let's figure out how much it costs to be you in your life right now. Fill out the Coin Calculator below with what you currently pay for living expenses, and be sure, if expenses are variable, to round up:

Coin Calculator

Monthly Expenses

Rent/Mortgage _____

Health insurance and other medical costs _____

Car payment _____

Car insurance _____

Phone payment _____

Gas, water, electric bills _____

Fuel _____

Estimated monthly groceries _____

Education (classes, lessons, etc.) _____

Entertainment (movies, shows, etc.) _____

Any additional monthly payments _____

Estimated extra monthly spending (clothes, gifts, etc.)

_____

EQUALS . . .

Total monthly expenses: _____

Now multiply those expenses by 15 percent (0.15). Why? You never know when extra expenses will come up in your life. The car registration is due. Your sister is getting married . . . in Hawaii. You have to get a cavity filled. You get the point. Surprise expenses come up for new budgeters on an almost monthly basis, so make sure to include these unforeseen expenses in your calculations.

Total monthly expenses _____

× 1.15 = _____

Total monthly income needed _____

If this seems like a large number, divide it into weeks.

Total monthly income needed _____

× 4 = _____

Total weekly income needed _____

You now officially have a great start on knowing what you need to earn to make ends meet. Hopefully, this seems like a reasonable number for you to earn to cover your expenses. If not, you should consider one of two things: either find ways to lower your expenses (get a roommate, take fewer classes, spend less on eating out) or raise your income (nab another side hustle or pick up extra hours at your current one).

DAY 2

Now that you know how much it costs to be you, let's compare your currently monthly income to your monthly expenses. Pull out your pay stubs for the past three months, or locate those figures on your handy-dandy banking app, and let's take an average of the three. Because you are more than likely a freelance-type person, your month-to-month income can vary. It's helpful to tally up and average a few months' income to get a good picture of how much dough you might bring in on a regular basis. Make sure that you're inputting these totals *after* taxes and payments to your representation (agents and/or managers). If you're a freelance worker who often works as an independent contractor (1099), I'm not going to spend a whole chapter lecturing about putting away money when you receive your checks, but you should definitely think about it. Those tax bills add up, and those IRS folks are no joke. Enter your actual monthly total income after taxes below.

Month 1 income _____

Month 2 income _____

Month 3 income _____

Three-month income total _____ / 3 = _____ Average monthly income

Now let's compare your actual average monthly income to your average needed monthly income from day 1.

Average monthly income _____

  − Average monthly income needed _____

  = Extra cash _____

Easy calculations, but what do you do if that number is negative? Or if it's very small? First things first: don't panic. Knowledge is power: you now know how much extra money you need to make to survive. That's a huge step (if you had not already made it). The next step is to find a way to make up that difference without interfering with your pursuit of your art. There are thousands of ways to make some extra cash these days, so if your extra cash tally is negative, take some time to go back to chapter 3, find a great additional side hustle, and go for it. As stated earlier, you could also consider lowering your spending. Perhaps you don't need that extra weekly voice lesson, or perhaps you could choose to spend some months shopping at Costco rather than Whole Foods. If you need any help coming up with ideas, just type "how to cut costs" into your favorite search engine, and you will find a plethora of suggestions, articles, and even videos. Hopefully, there is some solace in knowing that you are, by far, not the only person who has needed to cut spending to make ends meet.

DAY 3

Are we *still* on the money chapter? We sure are: money chapter hump day. We can't do a chapter on money in a workbook without talking about saving. I know, you're wondering, "How can I save money if I don't have a regular and steady income?" Great question. Yes, you should opt for a little more fluidity in your bank accounts than most people, in case of a rough audition season, injury, or other issue, but you should also think about saving your pennies as well. Because most performing artists work a lot of different gigs at a time, it's helpful to decide which income sources go where.

> Do not save what is left after spending, but spend what is left after saving.
> — Warren Buffett

For instance, Molly is a commercial dancer in Los Angeles who has just been hired as a backup dancer for an up-and-coming artist. Molly's new gig is sporadic, and her contract has her working six weeks out of the next three months (including a trip to Europe!). She also has a number of other gigs going on: she teaches two classes weekly at an LA dance studio, she is a hostess at a restaurant four nights per week, and she picks up other small gigs from time to time teaching private clients how to salsa dance. How does Molly figure out how much money to put in savings? She first completes the exercises from day 1 and day 2 and finds how much extra cash she will have on a monthly basis.

If that number is negative, again, Molly should find a different side hustle, pick up some extra shifts at the restaurant, or step up her game on advertising for new salsa clients. Madame Obvious says you shouldn't put money in savings when you're not making ends meet—obviously. If, though, the difference between her income and her expenses is positive, she should put 75 percent of that money in savings! Yes, 75 percent. Sure, she can put it *all* in savings, but it always helps to have a little extra cash around. If Molly happens to get an extra salsa client or two in the coming months, 100 percent of the money from that work should also go into savings. All things considered, if you're a freelance artist who's breaking even with your finances and you don't have extra cash to put into savings, don't fret. Just decide that when the next one-off gig comes up, you will put that money into a Roth IRA or index funds or a plain old savings account. Again, this isn't a money book, but if you were confused by the previous sentence, you should buy a money book and read it.

There are hundreds of ways to save your money, and we won't get into discussing them in depth in this book. Before you choose a place to put your extra moola, though, do your research. Perhaps you want to invest in a bond or you want to put your money in the stock market. Maybe you want to start a 401(k). These are all good options, and I won't tell you what to do other than *research your options* before you put your money somewhere. And make sure you ask about fees. And, for heaven's sake, google "compounding interest."

Let's first make a list of your "regularly scheduled" income sources:

_____

_____

_____

_____

_____

Make the decision that 100 percent of any income from any source other than the gigs you listed above should go directly into your chosen savings or investment account. Do not pass go, and make sure to collect your two hundred dollars. Now look back at the difference between your expenses and your income from yesterday. If that number is positive, put 75 percent of that amount into savings and enjoy spending the rest. The temptation is to say, "Oh, yay, extra money. It's time to celebrate and buy new shoes!" If you need new shoes, that's one story. Buy new shoes. If you don't, then you should put that extra dough where you can't touch it, because you will definitely need it for a rainy day. And it rains a lot in the performing arts industry.

Last task: set aside a time to decide where your extra cash goes. You can put it in a plain old savings account until you have the time to do your research, but just make sure you put your extra money somewhere other than your checking account, because it *will* disappear. Call up your bank and ask about starting a savings account (if you don't already have one) to hold your extra dough until you do your research. You might even be able to open one from your banking app without having to even leave your couch. And, by the way, it's okay if you only have five dollars in your savings account to start out. If you have one thousand dollars in the next year, you're doing better than 58 percent of Americans.[1]

DAY 4

Now let's have some fun with the future. Today you will be looking into an imaginary crystal ball to see yourself a year or two down the road, when you've booked a great gig, locked down a lucrative contract, or booked your long-term dream job. How does that change your finances? Look back at your research from day 3 of chapter 4, choose the job that you're most likely to nab in the next few years, check out the associated pay rate, and enter it in to your Coin Calculator. Assume your expenses are the same (don't buy your house in the Hamptons just yet) and recalculate your extra cash:

Average monthly income _____

− Average monthly expenses _____

= Extra cash _____

See how things can change quickly? You're rolling in dough! But wait! Before you head off to Bloomingdale's to nab that pair of Tom Ford sunglasses, put that extra cash into your savings account! Why? Let's do a little future-future calculation. Let's assume that you have been working your dream job as a lead in a feature film that is shooting in Atlanta. After two months of being on set in a different state, you've had to resign from your side hustle, and it takes you a little while to get back on your feet when you finish shooting and arrive back home. Let's assume that after you wrap your masterpiece, it takes you one month to get your side hustle(s) going again. What happens to your extra cash? Well, let's see:

Extra cash (from above) _____

− Average monthly expenses for one month _____

= Remaining extra cash _____

Uh oh. This chapter isn't as fun as you'd hoped. Here's the good news: it's better to plan now than to be surprised later, when you are working with real money. What if you happen to be unemployed for more than a month? Madame Obvious says, "Significantly less extra cash, that's what." The moral of the story is that your savings account can go down quickly when you're using it to pay your bills. Ideally, you won't have to use the money you've saved to keep the lights on in your fifth-floor walkup in Harlem, because you never have a lapse in income stream for the rest of your life. But if you need it, your savings account should always be there for you. This is also why it's imperative that you put money away into savings when you aren't working and that you have a flexible side hustle so you can connect the dots between Broadway shows, feature films, international tours, television series, dance company seasons, and any other lulls in the ebb and flow of the artistic lifestyle. The life of an artist is definitely not dull!

DAY 5

We've saved the most fun exercise for last. Today you're going to dream big and see what it costs. Spend fifteen minutes brainstorming what you want your life to look like in ten years. Do you want to own a boat? A cute house in Burbank? Do you want to travel the world for one month per year? Create your own record label? Do you want to have a kid or two? How about that new Porsche? Think big and put it all out there. List all of the things you hope to see in your future that might cost you some dough. (If you haven't read the Jim Carrey ten-million-dollar-check story, google it and use it as inspiration.) After you've listed your huge dreams, use your handy-dandy search engine to see how much they cost.

If your dreams don't scare you, then they're not big enough.
— Anonymous

Dream   Cost

_____   _____

_____   _____

_____   _____

_____   _____

_____   _____

_____   _____

_____   _____

Total cost to live large and in charge: _____

Now, divide that total cost by 120.

Total cost to live large and in charge / 120: _____

Why should you divide that number by 120? Because that is the number of months between now and ten years from now. If you save this amount per month for the next 10 years, you can attain all of that Real-Housewives-of-Beverly-Hills magic. Or, if you're a more philanthropically minded human, you can open your orphanage rather than fly to Fiji. Whatever floats your boat—or buys you one. While most people will not own an island in the Caribbean, it's helpful to see that almost anything is attainable.

Now look at your chosen field and see what you will need to accomplish to finance these huge dreams and make them come true. Do you need to not only join a dance company but also start your own as well? Do you need to not only book a lead on Broadway but also collect residuals from starring in a feature film? Do you need to write a book about being a backup singer as well as *being* a backup singer? Do you need to take your pirouettes to YouTube, gain a large following, and offer virtual coaching sessions to people around the world? Anything can happen if you let it (Mary Poppins, anyone?). Take a few moments to think big*ger* in terms of income from your art. How much will you make if you produce and sell a television show in addition to acting on TV? How much will you be paid for the advertisements on your super popular blog? Think outside the box and think big to support your long-term huge ideas.

Awesome source of income that will support my big dreams #1 _____

Compensation ($ earned doing it) _____

Awesome source of income that will support my big dreams #2 _____

Compensation ($ earned doing it) _____

Awesome source of income that will support my big dreams #3 _____

Compensation ($ earned doing it) _____

The point of this exercise is that if you're going to dream big, you also have to think big in terms of your career. Do you have to buy your own private jet and fly weekly to Peru for a massage overlooking Machu Picchu? No (but that's pretty awesome). The point is that there are many options in today's world of the arts and media, and there are very few boundaries. If you can think of it, it's highly likely that you can achieve it.

NOTE

1. Cameron Huddleston, "58% of Americans Have Less Than $1,000 in Savings, Survey Finds." Yahoo! Finance, May 15, 2019, https://finance.yahoo.com/news/58-americans-less-1-000-090000503.html.

Chapter Seven

Stand Out to Fit In

It's time to see how you and your talents fit into your future career plans and to determine what you can do to make yourself more perfect for your ideal job. This week, you'll spend time brainstorming what makes you great! You'll identify talents and physical traits you have that relate to your field. You'll take note of whether you happen to have great social skills, whether things about your "look" make you stand out, and you'll pinpoint anything else interesting or unusual about you that you can capitalize on to catapult your career. Are you an aspiring actor who's awesome at acrobatics? Or a singer who can harmonize with anyone? Or are you a dancer who can break-dance like no one else? Do you have crazy hair that makes you stand out? Are you exceptionally tall/short/pale/dark/geeky/extroverted/gutsy or anything else? Write it down. You never know when what makes you "weird" will actually be the thing that will get you your dream job. (We'll work on leveraging these things later, in the social media chapter.) Later in the week, you'll brainstorm the reciprocal. What skills do you still need to be competitive in your dream job? What could you learn that would help your side hustle?

You may be wondering why you should identify things that make you *different* from the people who are currently doing the jobs you want to be doing. You want to fit in to get the part, right? Not necessarily. The people who are currently doing the jobs you want to be doing are, well, already doing those jobs. If you look and act exactly like Robert Pattinson, why would you be hired to do a new feature film instead of him?

> Success in any endeavor depends on the degree to which it is an expression of your true self.
> — Ralph Marston

If you could be the evil twin of China Taylor (one of Janet Jackson's dancers), would you be hired for Janet's next tour instead of China herself? Probably not. You get the point. You're always going to be better at being *you* than at trying to be someone else. So let's explore what makes you different. What can you do that most people can't do? Or what is your special combination of skills and/or aspects of your appearance that would make someone notice you in a crowd?

A comedic actress who can play the accordion is significantly more interesting than just a plain comedic actress. Will this person always be hired to act and play the accordion simultaneously? Probably (and hopefully) not. But another key benefit of knowing what makes you special and sharing it with people in your industry is that it makes you memorable. A casting director for a television show that shoots in New York sees thousands of faces every day. It is not unheard of for an agent in Los Angeles to have thousands of submissions for a small role on a television show. And these submissions are just from people with agents; they don't include the people who will submit self-tapes who do not have representation. Of these thousands of faces, casting directors will *maybe* ask ten to fifteen to come in for an audition. It seems a little daunting, but if you happen to create a niche for yourself that is memorable, you will hopefully stand out from the crowd. And then, Madame Casting Directress will one day say something to her assistant to the tune of, "Remember that funny brunette with the accordion? Let's bring her in for this costar." And then you've gotten yourself into the room with casting and you can let your acting skills take it from there.

Once you identify what makes you stand out, it's time to find what could make you more employable. These days, artists do not do just their one kind of art in a vacuum. Working performing artists usually have multiple skills if they're among the privileged who are consistently working in the industry. If you've seen *The Band's Visit*, you know that those singers are not only singing but they're playing instruments as well. If you've ever seen a Cirque du Soleil–themed show on a cruise ship, you know those dancers are not just dancing but they're also singing and performing on aerial silks. Each new skill you add to your bag of tricks makes you more and more employable. Your extra skills don't necessarily have to be performance-based either. Perhaps you will find that it will help your career to learn to produce your own content or to spend some quality time on YouTube learning how to use Final Cut to edit your reel. Find the extra skills that will help you most to be uniquely you. Take into account the skills you already have and acquire new ones to help you speed along the path to achievement.

LET ME TELL YOU A STORY. . . .

I was a ballet dancer by trade. I danced in ballet companies, I trained at American Ballet Theatre school, and I regularly sewed pointe shoes instead of eating dinner. When I entered the musical theater scene, I stuck out in dance auditions like a sore thumb (largely because I wore a black leotard and pink tights). At my first audition for *My Fair Lady* at a lovely theater in New Jersey called Papermill Playhouse, I realized that one of these things was not like the other. Perhaps I stood out in the dance studio in a good way, but it was hard to tell. I noticed, though, as I continued to audition, that I stuck out when it came to the singing portion as well. As I listened through the door of the audition room, I heard dancer after dancer enter the room, sing "I Got Rhythm" or "All That Jazz," and then walk out in four-inch heels.

I began to get nervous. I was still in my ballet slippers and all I had brought with me to sing was "Think of Me" from *Phantom of the Opera.* To make matters worse, that was the only song I had sung in English for years. See, I had taken a lot of voice lessons in high school and college, but I had only been interested in opera. I haughtily considered myself a lyric coloratura and didn't prefer to sing things in English or notes "on the staff." For years, I had challenged myself to sing higher and higher notes and now, here I was listening to these throaty chorines belting out show tunes. I was at a loss. "Well," I thought, "I don't have any other choice and I'm not going to sing 'Happy Birthday' a cappella, so I might as well go for it."

Long story short: I got the job. I had good dance technique and a lot of personality, so I considered the dancing portion of the audition a success. However, that's not why I got the job. I found out later that the main reason I got the job was that the music director needed another soprano in the ensemble, and the score of the show was very high. Wait . . . I was offered a job in the dancing ensemble of a show because of my singing skills? This, to me, was odd, so I started to ask around about what kind of songs dancers sung at auditions and what was expected. It turned out that very few dancers at that time had classical training, and even fewer dancers sang high notes. Apparently, we dancer-sopranos were a pretty sought-after commodity in the regional musical theater circuit. A light went off—I had found my niche. I found a voice teacher who helped me not only build upon and show off my skills as a soprano but also fill in the gap in my training—learning to belt. After six months of weekly study, I had a book full of great songs like "Glitter and Be Gay" and "Gorgeous," to show off my high notes, as well as a few songs like "Don Juan" for me to pull out if asked to belt.

Less than two years after showing up at that first audition with no idea of how I fit into the musical theater world, I booked my first Broadway show. And then my next one. And the next one. And I didn't stop working for the next ten years. Was this all because I learned to capitalize on my particular mix of skills? No. Did it help? Sure did. The fact of the matter is that if you find the gaps in the market of your chosen artistic pursuit, and you and your talents can fill them, you will be likely to succeed. Similarly, if you find and fill the gaps in your skill set that will help you be a more well-rounded artist, you'll probably succeed as well. If you do both, I believe you can conquer anything.

It does not matter how slowly you go so long as you do not stop. — Confucius

DAY 1

Today you'll be writing down all of the things that set you apart from the other people who are in your chosen artistic field. We will be dividing your brainstorm into three categories: physical characteristics, skills and hobbies, and other attributes. You could list any physical attribute you have or anything you can do with your body such as flexible back, freckles, great style, piercings, or anything else. This can also include your "look" (think grunge Barbie, girly-girl style, or other things people might observe about you on first glance that would stand out). Your skills and hobbies can include things like running marathons, model car building, belting high notes, being great with animals, or other things you're good at or like to do. The last category, other attributes, leaves your brainstorming session open to anything else you can think of. Maybe you're from a small town in Iceland or you have ten siblings. Just write down anything you can think of that makes you stand out from the crowd. Set a timer for ten to fifteen minutes and get weird.

Physical Characteristics	Skills and Hobbies	Other Attributes

Your homework before tomorrow is to ask a few of your friends what *they* think stands out about you. You'll be surprised at how other people see us significantly differently from how we see ourselves. An outside perspective can often be very useful in many situations.

DAY 2

Hopefully, you now have a much fuller picture of what makes you . . . *you*. Or at least you now have one that is written in black and white. If you have any additional attributes that you gathered from your friends in your homework assignment, add them to your list from day 1. Today you will be choosing three of these attributes to apply in future chapters when you create your artistic style. You may even be able to combine a few of these at a later date. Say, for instance, you are a ballet dancer who loves fixing up motorcycles. Now, the combination of those two attributes will make for some memorable photos for your Instagram account. I'd definitely follow it! Or maybe you're an actor who loves fitness and animals. You can combine those. Workouts with your pet could be the next sensation and may attract eyeballs that will get you into the room with casting. But first, you'll simply choose three of the attributes that you listed above to put in your pocket for future planning. Consider how the differences you choose will set you apart from other dancers/singers/actors/performers and what the complementary other attributes might be. Perhaps even mentally look forward and consider what your overall style might be. List your three attributes below.

Attribute #1: _____

Attribute #2: _____

Attribute #3: _____

Now that you have decided on what makes you stand out, keep these three attributes at the top of your mind for the next few weeks. You will be thinking about how you can further define what makes you special, how that relates to your chosen career, and how it all fits together.

DAY 3

You will do a little more brainstorming today, but this time, you will be thinking about the opposite of day 1. What do you lack? What skills do you think you could add to the list of things you're already great at? What classes are offered in your community that you think might benefit you in your trajectory toward success? Remember, you may be employable as a singer, but you're even more employable if you're a singer who can tap-dance. Or a singer who can record and edit his or her own audio tracks. Or a singer who can also play the guitar. You don't have to know how to do everything, but you definitely should know how to do more than one thing. So what can you easily add to your bag of tricks that would make you a more employable artist in your field? Set a timer for ten to fifteen minutes and brainstorm all of the skills you might be able to add to your repertoire of talents to help you get a job. Remember to think outside the box; no idea is too outlandish. In fact, the more outlandish, the more memorable and unique.

_____

_____

_____

_____

_____

_____

_____

_____

_____

_____

_____

_____

_____

_____

_____

DAY 4

While you just may end up eventually procuring all of the skills from day 3 in your lifetime, it's undoubtedly overwhelming to think about all of them at once. So, today, you'll choose just one skill from your list to start adding to your mental cabinet of brilliance. Look back over your list of skills from day 3 and ask yourself, "What am I most excited about learning?" The last thing you want to do is embark upon learning something you're not passionate about. I can't stress this enough: don't pursue things that don't excite you. Ever. You should also ask yourself, "What is the low-hanging fruit?" Meaning, what is the easiest new skill that you could master that would give you the most bang for your buck? Some skills take years to master and others take weeks. Time is an important, nonrenewable resource of which we all have a limited supply. (That's your deep thought for the day.) If you can add a skill to your bag of tricks in less time than more, that's a great option to consider. A third thing you should consider is the financial cost you might incur when acquiring your new skill. Learning to juggle from YouTube videos is considerably less costly than learning how to golf. If you don't currently have a lot of cash, choose something that you can learn from friends or from online resources. To make your choice of what to study first a little simpler, you'll first narrow your choices down to three and then choose the best fit from there.

Additional skill #1 _____

Additional skill #2 _____

Additional skill #3 _____

Now set a timer and really consider each of these skills for three minutes each. Think of how long it will take to become proficient, how it will relate to your industry, and how much it will cost you. Then, after your nine minutes of consideration, make your choice.

Drumroll, please . . .

The skill I plan to add to my arsenal of amazingness is: _____

_____

DAY 5

No choice to move forward with any initiative is complete without an action plan. We all know that person who has been talking about starting a business or has been writing a book for years and still has not made any progress. Don't be that person. Thought without action is completely useless. Like a person who wants to save a million dollars but never deposits one dollar into the bank, the plans you make mean nothing unless you follow through with them. You may not have a lot of time to acquire your new skill, and that's okay. What you do consistently is more important than what you do on occasion. If you only have thirty minutes before you go to sleep to work on learning how to play the guitar, that's great. After three months, you will have been practicing guitar for forty-two hours. You'll be playing at a not-embarrassing level in six months and ready to show off your musical prowess in a year. Ensuring yourself a significantly higher chance of making more dough and getting hired more often for thirty minutes per day? That's a good deal.

Once you choose your skill to learn, you'll factor that cost into your Coin Calculator so you can make sure you keep that electricity on while you learn to play guitar. Here's an example from Ronald, who wants to be a comedic actor:

Artist: Ronald	Specialty: Acting
Skill I want to add:	Improvisation
How I plan to do it:	Classes at UCB in LA
I will do it:	3 hours per week
Additional cost:	$450 / 2 months
Brave skill debut:	Performance in 2 months

Now it's your turn:

Skill I plan to add to my arsenal of amazingness _____

_____

How I plan to learn it (i.e., lessons, from a friend, from videos, etc.)

_____

How long I will spend on this new skill: _____ hours per day / week (circle one)

Additional cost to pursue my skill: _____

Brave thing I will do to debut my new skill: _____

As you begin to recognize and capitalize on your inherent attributes and you cultivate additional supplementary skills to add to your bag of tricks, you will begin to stand out from the crowd. When you begin to stand out from the crowd (in a good way), people start to take notice. And when people start to take notice, you begin to get the opportunities that you have been waiting for. Learn to stand out so that you can fit into the world of working artists.

Chapter Eight

The Movie in Your Mind

This week, let's take a little break. Every day this week, you'll simply write out what a typical day in your future life as an artistic entrepreneur would look like. Get specific. For instance, you wake up in Paris and grab a chocolate croissant on the way to a put-in rehearsal for your international tour as a backup singer with an emerging pop artist. Or you wake up in Marina Del Rey, California, go surfing, grab a Starbucks, and drive to YouTube studios to star in the comedic web series that you wrote and star in. *Whatever*. Get as specific as you can. Where are you? What are you wearing? Who do you live with? Who are your friends? Do you drive, take public transportation, or walk? What is your role in whatever artistic project you imagine yourself doing? What do you do in your spare time during the day? Where do you eat dinner? When do you go to bed? Do you have a spouse/partner/roommate? Do you have children/pets/plants? You might want to look back at the different goals you set for yourself in previous chapters as well as your *why* and your *me* from chapter 2. Do you work on your side hustle during the day? Do you work on acquiring a new skill? Do you periodically talk to your mentor? It's okay if each day of the week is very different (I mean, they are, aren't they?) Have fun and don't just dream big . . . dream specific.

> It is not in the stars to hold our destiny but in ourselves.
> — William Shakespeare

This chapter is intentionally short on the explanation side because, for this week, you should be the one doing the explaining. Your future is legitimately a big blank page—as big and blank as the pages that follow. If you are a little intimidated by the bigness and blankness (and the entire world of choices) ahead of you, that's okay. You cannot dictate exactly when and how your future will play out, so consider this chapter an exercise in daydreaming. You do not have to describe one specific day in your future with exact accuracy; you will not be marked incorrect and get a bad grade. This is not a test. Imagining your future is like trying on a pair of shoes at the store. You don't usually buy shoes unless you try them on, and you don't know if they fit from just looking at them. You have to take time to imagine yourself in a future scenario to see if it's a path you are interested in pursuing. So, this week, *don't* set a timer and *do* spend as much (or as little) time as you want luxuriating in your fun and fabulous future.

DAY 1

Describe one day in your future in detail.

_____

_____

_____

_____

_____

_____

_____

_____

_____

_____

_____

_____

_____

_____

_____

_____

_____

DAY 2

Describe a different day in your future in detail. Choose either a different point in time or a different scenario.

_____

_____

_____

_____

_____

_____

_____

_____

_____

_____

_____

_____

_____

_____

_____

_____

DAY 3

Describe another different day in your future in detail. Choose either a different point in time or a different scenario.

_____

_____

_____

_____

_____

_____

_____

_____

_____

_____

_____

_____

_____

_____

_____

_____

_____

_____

In art, the hand can never execute anything higher than the heart can imagine. — Ralph Waldo Emerson

DAY 4

Describe a fourth different day in your future in detail. Choose either a different point in time or a different scenario.

_____

_____

_____

_____

_____

_____

_____

_____

_____

_____

_____

_____

_____

_____

_____

_____

_____

DAY 5

Describe the most perfect day you could ever imagine in your future.

_____

_____

_____

_____

_____

_____

_____

_____

_____

_____

_____

_____

_____

_____

_____

_____

_____

Aspects of these five days may not ever happen to you. And they also may *all* happen to you at some point. But hopefully, in creating different scenarios, you learned a little more about yourself and your preferences. And most important, you are now hopefully inspired by and excited about your brilliant future.

Chapter Nine

Creating Your Artist's Style

We talk about branding, essence, and style a lot these days in the world of the performing arts, but what do they actually mean? The definition of the word "brand" that Merriam-Webster provides is "a public image, reputation, or identity conceived of as something to be marketed or promoted."[1] So your "brand" is, in short, what you're putting out there in the world. It is the version of yourself that you cultivate and advertise to casting directors, directors, choreographers, music artists, viewers, readers, and networks to buy and/or hire. However, the word "brand" has been overused in today's society and has come to be viewed as disingenuous. The act of branding something can feel like putting a stamp or logo on something that is foreign to the actual thing you're marketing. So, for the purpose of this chapter, rather than creating a "brand" to put on like a Halloween costume, we will be exploring your genuine style. Your style is what is essentially *you*. We will work to define and refine your style and then find a way to use it to create an original niche in your industry.

> Style is something each of us already has, all we need to do is find it.
> — Diane von Furstenberg

Now, we all know that we are complex and multifaceted human beings who have hundreds of layers of talents, thoughts, memories, nuances, and conflicting wants and needs that can't be reduced down to a simple phrase like "badboy ballet dancer" or "quirky nerdy commercial actress." I also understand that most of us have the capability to play any role or take on any challenge. However, the goal of this chapter is to find out who *you* are and to make that recognizable and memorable. If you start with a simple concept that describes your essence, you can cultivate an audience and then slowly peel away the onion layers of your inevitably complex self for the world to enjoy.

A good example of an artist clearly defining her style is Lady Gaga. When Lady Gaga first stepped on the music scene, she was well known for her crazy outfits and dramatic makeup. From wearing a full white fur dress, leggings, and face mask to donning full combat gear with black lines on her face, to slipping on the iconic meat dress of 2010, she has worn pretty much everything and, in addition to creating great music, she became known as an icon of outlandish fashion. Almost ten years later, she has stripped off all of the makeup, eliminated the towering platform shoes, taken up acting, and she can regularly be seen on the red carpet looking, well, pretty normal. Does she still wear crazy outfits from time to time? Sure. The fact of the matter is that she initially caught our attention with her defined style and then, once she had solidified her place in her industry, she revealed other aspects of her talents, her personality, and her artistry.

Another thing you should consider when creating your style is your target audience. What kind of person will be excited by the work you are creating? Who will be looking for a "you-type" for their project? Are you creating music that will most likely be enjoyed by teenagers or are you dancing the ballet classics for a significantly more grown up crowd? Sometimes thinking of your artistry from the outside in helps to cultivate a clearer and more specific idea of your essence. The idea is to become known for the things that make you special. Remember when we brainstormed what makes you different in chapter 7? That will definitely come into play. And when you defined your *me* in chapter 2? That is important, too. The goal of all of this self-exploration in relation to branding and style is simple: your target audience is an exceptional bulls--t detector. If you create and market a brand or style that is not genuinely *you*, people will smell it a mile away and unfollow you faster than you can say Twitter. You don't (and shouldn't) need to be anyone else. If you find who *you* are and you share it genuinely, people will flock to your authenticity.

Think of all of the companies you know that you involuntarily recognize: Nike, Starbucks, McDonald's, Lululemon. They all have a specific logo, specific colors associated with their brand, and, most important, you know exactly what you're getting when you enter one of their establishments or purchase one of their products. We will be working this week to make your personal artist's style just as recognizable. You don't have to create a logo for yourself (your face should be your logo), but your audience should know exactly what they're getting when they see you. Are you the ephemeral ballerina who floats above earth and talks to the fairies? Or are you the gritty, sarcastic, and slightly dangerous lead singer of a punk band? Are you the geeky comedic actor who is exceptional at physical comedy? Or are you the down-to-earth spoken-word artist who isn't afraid to tackle controversial topics? The more specific you are when you define your style, the more recognizable you become.

If you're one of the many skeptics who don't believe you should have a "brand" if you're an artist, try naming one well-known artist who *doesn't* have one. It's hard, right? All people have a style, whether they like it or not. Sure, in a utopian society, art is all about the art and has nothing to do with the artist. That's not the case on this planet. You can either get specific about how you would like to put yourself out into the world or you can let the world decide your style for you. It's important to be proactive about cultivating how you and your work are being seen in the world. Even if you don't end up cultivating a style based on the exercises this week, you can still use them to do a little soul-searching to understand yourself a little bit better.

LET ME TELL YOU A STORY. . . .

I did a show at a large regional theater in Texas with a gentleman I will call Alan. Alan had one of the most gorgeous voices I had ever heard and was playing one of the lead characters in the musical we were performing together. After the show, people would literally throw themselves in front of our car as we were leaving to gush about the gloriousness of Alan's voice. Alan was cool and collected, and he always graciously deflected. At this time, Alan was a stout young blond man with kind eyes and puffy hair. He looked every bit the sweet and wholesome ingenue that he was playing in the musical.

Cut to a few years later when I saw Alan on my television screen on a reality show with black hair, black eyeliner, and black nail polish, wearing all leather and slaying a rock song. He still had that same uniquely pristine voice, but he had transformed his entire style to be specific and congruent with what he could do with his beautiful voice. His style was identifiable and cool, and the style I'd call rocker chic also fit his laissez-faire personality. After that reality show and the introduction of Alan, his talents, and his new style to the world, Alan has become a very well-known artist. Okay, I'll say it. He's famous. Did switching up his look make him so? Absolutely not. Alan was always destined for greatness in some venue, but I believe that the adoption of a particular style that was congruent with his talents and his personality helped catapult him to be the rock star that he currently is.

DAY 1

First, let's look back at the words you chose to describe yourself from day 5 of week 2. List your top three *me* words or phrases here:

1. _____
2. _____
3. _____

Next, look back at day 2 of week 7 and list your top three attributes:

1. _____
2. _____
3. _____

These are the six words you will use to start creating your specific description of your place in the arts industry. Set a timer for ten to fifteen minutes and start to brainstorm ways to combine as many of these aspects of *you* into one phrase or sentence.

_____
_____
_____
_____
_____
_____
_____
_____
_____
_____
_____
_____
_____
_____
_____
_____
_____

DAY 2

Next, you'll think about what you want to do in your industry. Do you want to make people laugh? Make people address tough subjects? Do you want to beautify the world? Bring joy to as many people as possible? Look back at your *why* from day 2 of week 2 for inspiration. If you know why you want to pursue a career in the arts, it's easier to discern exactly what you want to do. Set a timer for ten minutes and write out what you want to do in your industry:

_____

_____

_____

_____

_____

_____

_____

_____

Let's now put the two together into your statement of style. Start with the phrase that describes you, and add what you want to do as the second part of the sentence. For instance, "I am a smart, edgy, and uncompromising choreographer who wants to challenge audiences to view our planet's environmental issues through the media of dance and projection." Now, *that* is a pretty specific statement of style. Not only do we know who this person is as an artist and a human, we also know what he or she is working toward in the long run. Here's another: "I am a kooky, freckled best-friend comedian who wants to encourage families to laugh together to build closer relationships." Now your turn. Write your new statement of style below:

> My style is not that big. I wear heels, tight pants, and I wear diamonds.
> — Donatella Versace

_____

_____

_____

_____

_____

DAY 3

You know who you are, and you know how you want to change the world with your artistry and your humanity. Today we will be deciding who your target audience is. Can people of all shapes, ages, nationalities, genders, and demographics enjoy you and your art? Sure. Is it helpful to know what demographic is most likely to be your biggest fans? Absolutely. Think about the content you will be creating, the gigs you'll be pursuing, and your statement of style, from above. Now decide what type of person is most apt to be excited about you and your art, and fill in the blanks below to describe your ideal customer.

Age range: _____ years old to _____ years old

Gender: _____

Highest level of education: _____

Occupation: _____

Country of residence: _____

Yearly income: _____

Race or ethnic origin: _____

Your ideal customer is obviously not *every* person who will be interested in the things you create from now until forever, but this is a great way to verify that what you're putting out there is on target. If, for instance, your ideal customer is a thirteen- to eighteen-year-old girl who loves ballet, you are going to approach how you word things on a social media post significantly differently than someone whose audience is made up of twenty- to thirty-two-year-old, educated men who are interested in fitness.

At the end of the day, it's most important to be genuinely and uniquely *you* when making any decisions relating to your style. Defining your target audience is helpful, because it provides a great reference to have when you are making decisions in the future. If *you* as an artist feel strongly about something that isn't necessarily "on brand" with your "target audience," your *you* always trumps *them*. But knowing the type of person who consumes your "product" is a good tool for further defining the materials that you will put out into the world in the future.

DAY 4

Now that you have a good idea of what your style is and who will be seeking it out, let's decide how you will present yourself to the world. We all know that IKEA's brand is significantly different from Restoration Hardware's. But *how* do we know that? The stores both have different products, for sure, but we as consumers also see how each store presents itself on websites, publications, and social media. Today you will spend time treating yourself as you would any product in an exploratory marketing meeting. You will do some research first and then choose the colors that best represent you as an artist, the font or fonts that you think are "you," any images that specifically speak to your brand, and any other things that might be relevant to how you want to present yourself.

This may seem like an insignificant detail ("I just want to sing well and be on Broadway. Why am I spending my time choosing a font for my résumé?" you might say.) First, you have already chosen a font. Well, a font has been chosen for you. If you have a résumé, a website, or any kind of other presence online where you have written any text, you have a font. You just probably didn't intentionally choose it. Hopefully, this book will continue to help you be purposeful about even the small decisions that you make when it comes to your artistry. And, once you choose the look of your materials, you don't need to continue to choose every time you create a new piece of marketing material, update your website, or send out an e-mail update to your list of contacts (we'll talk about that in the next chapter).

People ask me where I got my singing style. I didn't copy my style from anybody. — Elvis Presley

LET ME TELL YOU A STORY. . . .

I created a Pinterest board for my writer's brand that helped me immensely. I just started compiling pictures of things that made me happy and that I felt were relevant to what I was creating. Eventually, a theme emerged, and I went from there. You can create a Pinterest board, a vision board, or go to Home Depot and gather paint sample cards—whatever works for you. Remember, your choices and your brand will change over time, but if you know who you are and what you're presenting to the world, you'll definitely be ahead of the game. Once you start to consider your style and pay attention to your preferences, most people find that it's actually fun. So let's have fun and make some decisions.

Your colors: _____

_____

_____

Secondary colors: _____

_____

_____

Your font: _____

Alternative font: _____

Overall vibe of your materials:

(Example: Gothic graphic novel feel—black and white, with orange accents and letters that drip off the page)

_____

_____

_____

_____

DAY 5

You've defined your style. Now you need to apply your ideas to your materials. Your website, your résumé, your business cards, your social media, and everything in between should tell the world who you are at first glance. If you don't yet have a résumé, business cards, or a website, that's great. You can start from scratch and create something awesome. If you do already have materials out there, list below the things that you have that you would like to update to reflect your redefined brand.

1. _____

2. _____

3. _____

4. _____

5. _____

Now set a time line for updating the materials above:

1. _____ will be updated by _____.

2. _____ will be updated by _____.

3. _____ will be updated by _____.

4. _____ will be updated by _____.

5. _____ will be updated by _____.

Finally, set an alarm in your phone or an appointment in your calendar for the dates listed above to make sure that you've followed through.

Defining your style may seem like a superficial product of today's follower-driven society. In some ways, it is. But it is a necessary step that every artist should take because, whether you have chosen it or not, you already have a style. Why not be purposeful about making sure that what you are putting out into the world is reflecting the true you? When people slap a "brand" on themselves that is incongruous with their true essence, we all can sense that it is not genuine. If you take time to be thoughtful about expressing your true self, you will be one step ahead of most artists.

NOTE

1. *Merriam Webster*, s.v. "brand," accessed October 11, 2019, https://www.merriam-webster.com/dictionary/brand.

Chapter Ten

Your Personal VIP List

You now have a few artistic career goals, one funtabulous side hustle, an inspiring mentor, a functional financial plan, a defined style, and some supplemental artistic skills in the making. It's time to add the *who* to your what, why, and how. This chapter helps you identify and expand the list of VIPs in your contact list (yes, your mom is one of those) and how they might help you move forward as an artist. If a tree (dancer) falls in the forest (wings) and no one is around to hear it . . . well, you know the saying. If you do brilliant things and nobody knows about them, you're doing a disservice to the world. You are likely pursuing a career as a performing artist because you want to share things with people: joy, beauty, music, inspiration, escape. All the "feels." If you keep them to yourself and don't share, you decrease your potential to make a positive impact on the planet. The larger your list of contacts, the more people you can share your art with, and the greater your impact on the world.

According to the *New York Times*, the average American knows about six hundred people.[1] Let's assume you're average (you're probably not) and that you're an agreeable person for whom a majority of people would do a favor (you probably are). Let's also say that you're a singer-songwriter and you just released a new single that you want to promote (congratulations!). If four hundred of those six hundred people you know agree to share a social media post with twenty of their friends, your new release has just received 16,000 eyeballs (assuming all of your friends have two of them). Maybe only five percent of those folks actually buy your new single, but that's still four hundred singles sold with one mass e-mail request to your contact list.

The currency of real networking is not greed but generosity.
— Keith Ferrazzi

That's four hundred people you have had the opportunity to influence with your music. And that's even assuming that the people your original group of contacts shared your song with did not share it with any of their friends, which would have yielded even more single buyers. These days, it's significantly easier to keep in touch with people and cultivate relationships than back in the dark ages before the Internet and social media. It can also be overwhelming and difficult to know where to start to create an audience for your work. That's why you have this book! At the end of this week, you will have a handy-dandy blueprint for getting your contact list started as well as a plan for how to update people on what you've been creating.

You will not only compile a list of people with whom you will share updates and information, but you'll also choose a few "power players" you might not know yet and will want to add to your list (don't forget to include your mentor from chapter 5). Do you have an aunt who lives in New York you don't talk to often? Don't be afraid to send her an e-mail asking if she knows any Broadway actors who are interested in mentoring up-and-coming talent. Do you want to be the next Katy Perry? Search (and ask around) for the best managers for new talent and start reaching out. Managers and agents can sound scary, but their *job* is to find and support new talent. *That's you*! At the end of this week, you will also have filled out a chart with twenty VIPs with whom you'll cultivate new relationships and keep in touch. New friends equal new opportunities.

LET ME TELL YOU A STORY. . . .

I did a production of *Beauty and the Beast* in Utah with a lovely gentleman named Kraig. Kraig was a fun-loving and hilariously witty character actor with an impish smile, and we got along immediately. We spent the entire run giggling our way through shows and exploring the sights in Salt Lake City. After that show finished, I decided to keep in touch with Kraig. I added him to my contact list and reached out periodically to grab lunch or take a walk around Central Park. When I moved to Los Angeles many years later, I still kept in touch, and when Kraig came to visit LA, he invited me to dinner with one of his choreographer friends.

Now, the evening he invited me to dinner was the end of an *exhausting* week at my side hustle job, I was nursing a sinus infection, and I hadn't slept the night before. As much as I loved Kraig, the last thing I wanted to do was go out and meet new people. After much deliberation, I finally decided to join them so that I could expand my list of contacts on the West Coast (and so I could see my buddy). It turns out that Kraig's friend was absolutely delightful. Peggy and I felt like we had been friends for years. We laughed about mutual friends, told dance stories from crazy auditions, and all around hit it off. I left that evening feeling very happy that I had decided to go out despite my illness and fatigue. Guess what? I kept in touch. I wanted to keep in touch with Peggy because she was a really fun new friend, but I also knew that she was (and still is) a consistently working choreographer. Two years later, Peggy called and offered me a role in the musical she was choreographing in Los Angeles. The moral of the story is that you never know when you will be the right person in the right place at the right time. How do you put yourself in a position to be in the right place at the right time? Put yourself in a lot of places a lot of different times. Meet people, create relationships, and then (most important) continue to maintain and nurture those relationships so that you're at the forefront of people's minds when they encounter an opportunity for which you would be suited.

Adding a person's information to your list of contacts is pointless if you do not maintain a relationship with that person. If you meet people in your industry, you should plan to continue to reach out to them after your initial point of contact. Now, this only applies if you like the person. Please don't maintain a relationship with a subpar person for the sake of keeping a contact on your list. It's not worth it. And, chances are, the person you don't get along with will sense that you don't get along and will think it's odd that you're trying to continue a relationship that doesn't work.

Speaking of genuine relationships, I must offer a quick piece of advice. As you build your network of friends, fans, and acquaintances, you *must* be genuine. If I've said it once, I've said it a million times: people are exceptional bulls--t detectors. We all know when someone wants something from us and is using us to get it. Don't be that person. Take the time to create a *genuine* relationship with as many people as possible. Ask how *they* are. Comment on *their* events and successes. And share some of your own as well. The point is to genuinely try to add value to people's lives. Nobody likes a virtual moocher; you want your contacts to be happy to receive an update from you and happy to share your accomplishments with their contacts because they care about you and you care about them. Incidentally, if you haven't read any of Gary Vaynerchuk's books, he is a master at the art of relationship creation via digital media; I highly recommend nabbing one of his books or listening to his podcast. Gary Vee, do you want to help spread the word about this book? (See what I did there?)

Effective networking isn't a result of luck—it requires hard work and persistence.
— Lewis Howes

DAY 1

You know that it's all about who you know. Today you will be creating a list of your current contacts, from the people who know and love you to the people who only know of you. If you haven't been living in a cave, you probably know a lot of people, and this exercise will take a long time. I encourage you to continue to add to your list of contacts as you remember people you know and as you meet new people in your life. If you do this correctly, you will be starting a list of contacts today that you can keep and grow for the rest of your life. Think of *everyone*; they all matter. Your high school choir teacher, your yoga teacher, the mom of the kid you babysat, your local librarian, your aunts, uncles, cousins, and long-distance relatives—add them to your list! Similar to your mentor table, you will also be adding a contact date to each person so that you know when to reach back out if it's been a while. You can also select all of your e-mail addresses and send an invitation to your upcoming show in just a few clicks of the mouse. So let's get started. Set a timer for fifteen to twenty minutes and start filling out the boxes in the table below. (Eventually, you will probably want to re-create this in a spreadsheet format to keep on your personal computer.)

Name	E-mail	Social Handle	Contact #1	Contact #2	Contact #3
Mary Actorfriend	maryactorfriend@ gmail.com	@actormary	10/3 Update e-mail	10/29 Invitation to my show	11/4 Kitten article

DAY 2

You will hopefully continue to add to the list from day 1 for the rest of your career, so take the time to trick it out. Make it colorful and format it in a way that makes you happy so that you will use it more often. Today you will focus on the people you eventually want to add to this list of contacts. Whom do you want to someday know and be able to reach out to in the industry? What are the relationships you want to cultivate with established directors, composers, choreographers, producers, casting directors, and writers? This should be your networking wish list. However, it doesn't have to be super specific or filled with famous people. You can even include "the casting director for singers for Celebrity Cruises" because you know from chapter 4 that you can easily do some focused research to find out more information about this person. Set a timer for fifteen to twenty minutes and list all of the people you would like to eventually add to your table from day 1. As you get to know each of these contacts, move them from this list to your networking table from day 1.

People I would like to someday add to my list of contacts:

_____

_____

_____

_____

_____

_____

_____

_____

_____

_____

_____

_____

_____

_____

_____

_____

DAY 3

Today you're going to make a list of people you don't know . . . but who know you. If the first thing that came to your mind is a stalker on *Forensic Files*, you're probably evolved enough to survive an apocalypse. Fight-or-flight instincts? Check! But there are more than likely a few people who know *of* you and would be interested in supporting you and your endeavors. Your mom's sister's daughter who is in middle school and wants to be you when she grows up, and anyone who follows you on social media you don't know are prime targets to add to the list below (or to the table you created on your own from the first day of this week).

The point of having a comprehensive list of contacts within your industry (and supporters outside your industry) is to be able to easily keep in contact with everyone. Why do you want to keep in contact with the people you know? So that you stay at the forefront of their minds in a crazy, crowded digital world of distraction. According to a *Forbes* magazine article, "The average sale requires seven to 10 touches with the brand before a potential buyer converts into a customer."[2] Essentially, that is what you want to do. People who could potentially hire you or recommend you for a job in your field are your "customers" (once converted) and the people you should work to "touch" seven to ten times in order to solidify your place in their minds. Heck, in today's age of social media, a like, a follow, a comment, or a retweet is a small sale, so your potential customers don't even have to be in your field. Set a timer for fifteen to twenty minutes and list all of the people you don't know. You will learn a little more about what to do with all of these contacts on days 4 and 5.

_____

_____

_____

_____

_____

_____

_____

_____

_____

_____

_____

_____

_____

_____

DAY 4

Now that you have a *lot* of contacts, let's decide what to do with them. First, if you have not done so already, check in with the people on your list from day 3 and see if they are interested in keeping up with you and receiving periodic e-mails about what's up in your professional career. (It should go without saying, but please do *not* include any creepers or weird-seeming folks on this list.) When these folks reply in the affirmative, move them from your day 3 list to your day 1 table. Likewise, as you develop a relationship with your as-pirational contacts from day 2, also move them to your list from day 1 (if you do this, congratulations!). Get it? Over time, your list from day 1 will become your official

networking resource list. This is the list of people you will contact if you have extra tickets to your shows, if you book a feature film, and if you have a new blog/website/podcast/single/cabaret/short film/book. Spend some time today working on your of-ficial list (from day 1) and list below, in order of importance, the contacts you will work to move from your day 2 and day 3 lists to your master networking contact list.

1. _____

2. _____

3. _____

4. _____

5. _____

6. _____

7. _____

8. _____

9. _____

10. _____

DAY 5

You've got a list! Now how do you use it? Great question. The short answer is: *very carefully*. Time is the only nonrenewable resource in our lives, and the simple action of messaging, texting, e-mailing, or calling someone takes away time of theirs that they will never get back. That's a very dramatic way of saying that you should only contact people on your list when you have something to say! Keeping in touch for the sake of keeping in touch is not useful. And it also can make you seem slightly desperate. Here are the rules of networking according to this book:

- Use your contact information sparingly. Ideally, you only contact people once every two or three months. You should also be very protective of this information. Do not share personal contact information unless you have the person's permission.
- When possible, your communication should be personalized. If you plan to send out a newsletter-type update to your entire list of contacts every three months, that's great. But take the time to send at least a few sentences that are tailored to your recipient along with that newsletter.
- Again, do *not* send any communication that does not *say* anything. You don't have to just have won a Tony Award to let people know you are doing something useful for your career, but you do need to send some kind of update. You can let people know you've just started studying aerial silks, and include a picture of you doing the splits in the air, or that you've been volunteering to sing for the elderly. Heck, you can even let people know that you've just gotten a puppy and have found your new pet to be the best scene partner for your monologue practice in the world. Incidentally, "I got new headshots" is not a good enough reason to e-mail your entire contact list. But "I got new headshots, a new agent, and I have a new e-mail address"? Absolutely.
- Keep it short. If you have one awesome thing to tell people, give specific details, add a picture, and wrap it up. If you haven't gotten in touch in a while but you don't have anything pivotal going on, get creative, get personal, add value, and let your contacts know how you are working to make something happen. Again, though, the shorter the better.
- Real talk: I don't think many of us stopped preferring picture books when we became adults. Probably because, according to MIT News, your brain can identify objects seen for only thirteen milliseconds.[3] That's a *lot* faster than reading about something. Perhaps a picture is truly worth a thousand words. So, if you can include some kind of picture (preferably of you) in your communication, chances are that even if your contacts don't have time to read the whole e-mail or message, they will clock the picture (in thirteen or more milliseconds), recognize your face, and instantly put your mug in their brain for future consideration (whether they like it or not).
- Offer value! If you know what a contact likes, send a fun bit of information about that subject (i.e., "I remember that you collect Persian scarves and I found a great lady at the Burbank farmer's market that sells them! Here's a picture"). Or you can offer something of value that you've been working on ("I've been creating a

new set of workout plans. I've attached a few in case you are interested in taking a look!"). Give tips, tickets, codes to see your films for free, and fun new bits of information when you can. This is not what all your communication should be about, but a little tip, gift, coupon, or offer never hurt anybody.

Now that you know *how* to network, let's get going! Make sure to enter the dates when you have communicated with your contacts onto your table so you make sure not to wait too long (or not long enough) before getting in touch again. Do you have something going on right now that you would like to let people know about? Get started! Write a (short) message (with a picture), select all of the e-mails from your table that you would like to let know about this, and commence networking!

NOTES

1. Andrew Gelman, "The Average American Knows How Many People?" *New York Times*, February 18, 2013, https://www.nytimes.com/2013/02/19/science/the-average-american-knows-how-many-people.html.

2. Ryan Robinson, "Five Ways Sales Has Changed in Recent Years (and How to Adapt)," *Forbes*, March 13, 2019, https://www.forbes.com/sites/ryanrobinson/2019/03/13/how-sales-has-changed/#d0aed253985a.

3. Anne Trafton, "In the Blink of an Eye," MIT News, January 16, 2014, http://news.mit.edu/2014/in-the-blink-of-an-eye-0116.

Chapter Eleven

Do What You Do Best

You've spent the last ten chapters gathering good ideas to get your performing arts career in gear, so this week, we will refocus on doing what you do best. No matter what you do—singing, dancing, acting, performance art, or anything else—natural talent is useless without practice. No amount of business savvy, brainstorming, or baby-I-was-born-this-way talent makes up for hours in the dance/acting/recording/art studio. You've probably already put in the magical ten thousand hours to hone your craft (thank you, Malcolm Gladwell), but have you gotten specific about when and what you will practice? It's one thing to say, "I'm going to practice singing this week as much as I can." It's a whole other thing to say, "I'm going to practice singing on Monday, Wednesday, and Friday this week from 9 a.m. to 10:30 a.m., and I'm going to bring new music every day to practice my sight-reading." That second statement? That's the kind of thing Olympic athletes say. The first statement? That's what almost everyone else says.

... If people knew how hard I worked to get my mastery, it wouldn't seem so wonderful at all.
— Michelangelo

Like an Olympic athlete, you hopefully have a specific long-term goal (e.g., booking a television series, singing on Broadway, touring the world to promote your new album), but we all know we have to break out long-term goals into short-term practice goals.[1] What most people don't do, though, is create specific goals for every time they practice. Sure, it's always beneficial to go to a dance class, because you will inevitably become an incrementally better dancer every time you take class. But imagine how much more you will improve if you set a specific goal for yourself *within* that dance class. If you do this once, any difference between you and any other artist might not be discernible. If you do this every time you practice or take a lesson or class, those incremental improvements will make for a significantly more successful career.

Another good reason to actively choose what you want to work on in your practice or lessons is that it makes you more aware of yourself and how you approach your art. There are very few situations in life where it will behoove you to be *less* aware, and honing your skills is not one of them. Sometimes we practice just to enjoy doing what we love doing, and that's okay (and can be useful to you in many ways). However, when you focus on *how* you are practicing rather than just going through the movements, you not only can shift your attention to what aspect you are working on in that session but you also will inevitably be more present in your work in general.

Here are some specific ideas for what to think about improving in addition to taking a lesson/class/rehearsing a scene:

- Improve your performance quality
- Be a better listener
- Work on flexibility (both physical and mental)
- Focus on quicker "pickup" (sight-singing, picking up choreography, memorizing lines, etc.)
- Be a clearer storyteller
- Breathe more often and more deeply
- Connect more purposefully with other humans
- Work on dynamics/nuance/specificity
- Be more free and/or take more risks (artistically)

Even if you aren't completely successful when attempting to improve some part of your art, you are still one step above the rest because you made a concerted effort to be more present in your education. This alone will set you apart from the masses.

Additionally, if you don't track your progress, one of two things happens: you either don't realize how far you've come, or you don't recognize when your progress has stalled. Keeping a practice log is an important step to maximizing your practice and class time, because it is difficult to improve upon what you don't measure in the first place. You may think you will remember what you did, but why take up prime brain real estate to remember, say, whether you could sing a high C two months ago? You have other important things to think about, and if you keep a log of your sessions, you can free up that brain space for something else worthy of contemplation. Writing things down takes thoughts out of the pinball machine that is your brain and puts them in black and white. This action alone can help relieve some general anxiety and uncertainty. It can also clue you in when the approach you are taking isn't so successful. So, this week, you will schedule when and what you'll practice and keep a log of how it went and what you can do to improve. We will take a break from our regularly scheduled exercises to refocus on the main thing that will make you successful: passionate hours of practice doing your craft.

LET ME TELL YOU A STORY. . . .

This story is not a do-it-like-I-did kind of story. Consider this a more cautionary tale. When I was studying to be a ballet dancer, I operated under the principle of "more is more." I took ballet classes morning, noon, and night. And then I would take an extra class after my night class. I volunteered to teach at different ballet schools around my town so I could take even more classes. When I wasn't sleeping, I was in some ballet class somewhere. However, I didn't get specific about what I was working on. I listened to teachers and took the corrections I was given, but I was not purposeful about my practice. I didn't, say, think of working on my turnout or improving my placement. I just took class. Incessantly. And guess what? I didn't progress that much. First of all, I was too tired to focus most of the time. Second, I was simply going through the movements of ballet class without really working on one thing.

One of the things that deterred me from trying to work on one thing at a time was, sadly, my pride. I wanted every ballet teacher to like me all the time, and I thought

Quality is much better than quantity. One home run is much better than two doubles.
— Steve Jobs

that if I focused on one specific thing in class, I might not be as good as I could be in the moment for them. Interestingly, there actually is some truth to this kind of thinking. Much like cleaning out a closet, sometimes things have to get messy before they get clean again. If you are working on one aspect of your craft, it's okay for some of the other aspects of your work to fall by the wayside. But, unlike young Michelle, you sometimes have to put your pride aside in order to do it. Take the time to break down what you are working on and how you are improving it, and eventually, you will notice that you are miles ahead of where you were.

DAY 1

Today you'll do some focused work on your craft. Remember, you don't have to pay hundreds of dollars for coaching or lessons or haul yourself to a class across town to complete this mission. For *most* of the performing arts, you can work on aspects of your artistry at home. If you're an actor who can't afford an acting class, invite a friend over to work on a scene and cook ramen for the friend as a thank-you. If you're a singer, slay those scales, record yourself on your phone, listen back, and start over. If you're a dancer, search the Internet for conditioning exercises, lay a yoga mat out next to your bed, and get going. You may need to get creative, but there is *always* a way to improve on the cheap. So, let's make some decisions and get to practicing.

Today I will work on my art from _____a.m./p.m. to

_____a.m./p.m.

I will work specifically on _____.

Practice log:

Things I did that I would like to do again:

_____

_____

_____

_____

_____

Ways that I can continue to improve:

_____

_____

_____

_____

_____

DAY 2

In your practice session today, you will keep working on the same specific thing you did on day 1. Sometimes it takes a little while for concepts to take hold. You can't just do something once and expect your brain to rearrange its synapses immediately. It takes time—a lot of time, in fact. On average, it takes sixty-six days for a new behavior to become automatic. It takes even longer to form a habit.[2] So practicing one thing once, while incrementally helpful in the development of your art, is not the most effective way to get better. Try scheduling chunks of multiple months during which you will focus on improving one specific aspect of your craft.

Today I will work on my art from _____a.m./p.m. to

_____a.m./p.m.

I will work specifically on _____.

Practice log:

Things I did that I would like to do again:

_____

_____

_____

_____

_____

Ways that I can continue to improve:

_____

_____

_____

_____

_____

> If a man is called a streetsweeper, he should sweep streets even as Michelangelo painted, or Beethoven composed music, or Shakespeare wrote poetry. He should sweep streets so well that all the hosts of heaven and Earth will pause to say, "Here lived a great street sweeper who did his job well."
> — Martin Luther King, Jr.

DAY 3

Make one incremental change in your work today. Perhaps you change the room in which you write your screenplay, the way you sit when you practice the guitar, the wall you face when you're dancing. Maybe you lightly jog while working on the sixteen-bar contemporary musical theater cut that you are perfecting for your next audition. Changing one small thing in your regularly scheduled practice sessions can either throw you off a bit (in which case, it's better to be thrown off now rather than in a high-stakes situation) or it can give you a fresh perspective that will inspire new ideas. The idea here is to make things hard for yourself before outside forces make things hard for you. (Incidentally, has anyone heard the rumor that Beyoncé sings all of her albums on a treadmill to improve her stamina?)

Today I will work on my art from _____a.m./p.m. to

_____a.m./p.m.

I will work specifically on _____.

Practice log:

Things I did that I would like to do again:

_____

_____

_____

_____

_____

Ways that I can continue to improve:

_____

_____

_____

_____

_____

_____

DAY 4

In your practice/creation session today, keep that change you made in day 3. The more you can throw new things at yourself and then work to take each new change in stride, the more prepared you will be for any bumps in the road in the future.

Today I will work on my art from _____a.m./p.m. to

_____a.m./p.m.

I will work specifically on _____.

Practice log:

Things I did that I would like to do again:

_____

_____

_____

_____

_____

Ways that I can continue to improve:

_____

_____

_____

_____

_____

Your homework for tomorrow is to invite one person that you trust to your practice/creation session on day 5.

DAY 5

It is important that you become accustomed to performing your art in front of other people. If you're reading this book, you're probably a dancer, actor, singer, or some other kind of artist who does things for or in front of other people. These art forms are not inherently solitary endeavors. Even if you're a writer, you may one day be welcomed into a writers' room, and it's better to become comfortable working with others earlier than later. So today you'll practice/create for and with a friend. It will probably be awkward, and you might feel a little (or massively) embarrassed. That's great. Why? The more awkward and embarrassed you feel now, the less awkward and embarrassed you will feel in the future when you are put in a professional situation or audition. Ask your friend to participate in the session; invite feedback, talk about strategy, and *listen*.

Today I will work on my art from _____a.m./p.m. to

_____a.m./p.m.

I will work specifically on _____.

Practice log:

Things my friend liked that I did:

_____

_____

_____

_____

Ways my friend feels I can continue to improve:

_____

_____

_____

_____

Feedback from friends can be tough to hear, but the more you get used to hearing feedback and incorporating it, the better. Your friend may be just plain wrong in what he or she suggests in relation to your session, but this kind of thing happens in the professional world often. If a producer of a commercial does not believe your very genuine acting, then you need to switch up what you're doing or be replaced. Similarly, if you're dancing in the front line of the corps de ballet of *Swan Lake* and the ballet master tells you that your arabesque is too high, you will have to fix it. This exercise is more centered around getting you to become more comfortable performing in front of other people and less about exactly what your friends say. Having said that, a little feedback from an outside perspective never hurt anybody.

NOTES

1. T. Jorgenson, "6 Things We Can Learn from Olympic Athletes," Mayo Foundation for Medical Education and Research, February 9, 2018, https://dahlc.mayoclinic.org/2018/02/09/6-things-we-can-learn-from-olympic-athletes.

2. James Clear, *Atomic Habits: An Easy and Proven Way to Build Good Habits and Break Bad Ones* (London: Random House Business Books, 2018).

Chapter Twelve

Dress the Part

This week you'll begin to develop the habits you will need when you're a successful working artist (or the ones you should maintain if you already are). You'll act, dress, speak, and imagine yourself already having your dream career. In short, this week, you'll "fake it 'til you make it." What if you don't have any red carpets to attend? What if you don't have anything to do other than just take a dance class? How about dressing for that dance class as if you were going to an audition? First, if you're not in your pajamas, you'll be Instagram-photo-worthy (see chapter 15), and second, you'll figure out if that outfit/look even works for an audition. (Anybody ever worn a shirt that looks cool but you can't raise your arms?) If you're a singer, you can spend this week treating yourself as if you're singing a grueling eight-show week. Get good rest, hydrate, warm up your voice, go to the gym. The idea is that if you imagine you're working in your ideal career, and you create habits that will support your longevity while you're in that career, those habits will be easier to keep when you've finally made it to the top.

Perception is everything, both from the outside in and from the inside out. While humans may have active imaginations, they rarely use their imaginations in relation to other humans' abilities. This is why television shows like *The Voice* are so popular. It's a big surprise reveal moment for everyone to see the geeky-looking guy sing like Pavarotti, because we all judge books by their covers no matter how often we say we don't. This judgment is not always bad, though, because our assumptions often save us time and make our lives easier. According to peak performance coach Max Weigand, "Our brains are designed to conserve energy, and the best way to do that is to run the same mental loops over and over again so you don't have to spend precious energy on active thinking."[1] That makes sense from a brain-efficiency standpoint, but it doesn't help you out from the imagine-me-playing-Curly-in-*Oklahoma!*-even-though-I'm-wearing-a-tank-top-and-refuse-to-take-out-my-nose-ring standpoint.

Your brain is all about increasing its efficiency. If you've ever passed a restaurant that looked dirty from the outside, you've probably made the wise assumption that eating there might give you food poisoning. You move along to another, cleaner establishment. This is usually a quick decision but one that you perceive will keep you safe and upchuck-free. But what if that restaurant was run by a Michelin-star chef and simply needed a fresh paint job? Your seemingly wise choice has just turned into a missed opportunity. You get where I'm going here, right? You are the restaurant that might need a new coat of paint, and one of the easiest things you can do to boost your career is model your now self to be your future self. Dressing and acting the part are a quick and easy way to take a large leap forward in your career.

We all may judge the restaurant by its exterior, but what's also interesting is that the proverbial restaurant has also been proven to judge *itself* by its exterior. You can pretend your way into believing something. Embarrassingly, our brains are quite easy to fool, even if we are completely aware that we're trying to fool ourselves. Dress a little girl in a party dress, and she immediately begins spinning and curtsying as if she were a part of the royal household. Whether it's true or not, if you tell yourself enough times that you are smart/dumb/entitled/worthy/unworthy/ugly/beautiful/tired/competent, you *will* begin to believe it. So why not tell yourself that you already are your future self even if you don't currently have the job or recognition that you hope and plan to eventually have? You have nothing to lose.

The one caveat here is that you cannot sacrifice your humility in pursuit of your persona. Nobody likes a cocky or aloof artist and, if you remember from week 10, relationships are one of the most important aspects of creating a career with any longevity. If you act like a diva on one project, you'll likely not be hired on the next. So while you are faking until you make it and modeling your actions and outward appearance after a successful artist, you should also be gracious about it. Incidentally, the *most* successful artists are those humans that are present, giving, kind, and collaborative. If you ever need an example of how to be confident, successful, and gracious, just look at Will and Jada Pinkett Smith and family.

Before I go on stage I pretend that everyone loves me. — Adam Levine

DAY 1

Before you model your ideal self in your future career, let's revisit who that future person is. Spend some time thinking about how you present yourself and how you interact with others in your artistic endeavors. Start by reminding yourself of your *me* words or phrases and list them below:

1. _____

2. _____

3. _____

Next, you'll spend some time brainstorming how your *me* will relate to your work in your field in the future. For example, if one of your *me* words is "sophisticated," that should translate to how you choose your clothes for your recording session/audition/rehearsal/agent meeting. If one of your phrases is "knows what she wants," then you'd better put on your confidence coat before you head out in the morning. Remember, there is no wrong answer in this brainstorm.

The ways you choose to relate your actions and appearance to your *me* words is your prerogative and part of what makes you a unique and worthy human. Set a timer for ten to fifteen minutes and get going on creating your future self.

Me word or phrase #1:

_____

How this will manifest itself in my actions and appearance:

_____

_____

_____

_____

_____

_____

Me word or phrase #2:

_____

How this will manifest itself in my actions and appearance:

_____

_____

_____

_____

_____

_____

_____

Me word or phrase #3:

_____

How this will manifest itself in my actions and appearance:

_____

_____

_____

_____

_____

_____

DAY 2

Now, it's time to dress the part. Spend some time in your closet choosing outfits that say, "I am a successful actor/dancer/singer/performer." If you don't have a lot of clothing options, this does not give you permission to go directly to Saks or Bloomingdale's for a shopping spree (unless you've got a lot of dough lying around). Start by choosing options out of what you have and then check apps like thredUP and Poshmark to supplement remaining items on the cheap. Or, if you have a lot of stylish friends, you might consider having a clothing swap (this is generally more a lady thing than a gentleman thing, but it's very effective). Remember, while you're choosing your successful artist "look," that you will be going to different types of events. Rehearsals, meetings, and screenings all require different looks, and you should plan to represent yourself appropriately and fabulously at all of them.

Opportunity is missed by most people because it is dressed in overalls and looks like work.
— Thomas Edison

You might think that this is a silly exercise and that you would rather be dancing/singing/acting/producing/creating than scouring your closet to dress for the career that you may not have yet. In truth, it is a little bit superficial . . . on the surface. However, the goal is to set yourself up to *feel* different and to become even more confident in your inevitably successful future. One of the most useful tools to help you feel more successful is to dress for it. People judge you and size you up in your first five to seven seconds of interaction. (It's sad but true.) It's also been proven that if you are dressed well, you're more likely to be confident and detail-oriented.[2] Does this mean that you need to wear a three-piece suit to the grocery store? No. However, a sensible Lululemon athleisure outfit along with clean I'm-going-to-the-gym-after-this-grocery-trip grooming can go a long way.

If you're one of those people who doesn't know (or care) about clothing, that's okay, too. Find a friend who does care and ask that friend to help you assemble your looks. Chances are, he or she will leap at the chance to play a version of Barbie doll dress-up party with a live human being. (Don't forget to make sure that friend is on your networking sheet, and consider how you might add value to his or her projects in the future as a thank-you for styling you.)

For today's task, take the time to choose five to seven looks for different occasions that make you feel stylish, successful, and confident, and then *take photos* of them so that you can easily and quickly re-create the fabulousness. If you need some inspiration, search for the "Cher's Closet" clip from *Clueless* on YouTube. Save your photos to a folder in your phone and then add and subtract from them as you come up with new ideas for looks or retire your least favorites.

DAY 3

Now that you have an arsenal of outfits (bet you never thought that would be a task in this book), you're going to add the drama (or lack thereof) to your day. Today you'll be acting the part of your future self. First things first, write down your plans for today, including scheduled items, such as "3 p.m.—Voice Lesson," and more casual, everyday things, like "Go to the grocery store."

_____

_____

_____

_____

_____

_____

_____

_____

Then, next to your plans, write how you plan to feel and act while doing each of your daily tasks. At your 3 p.m. voice lesson, you can choose to be confident in making mistakes because in your mind, you are already the vocal diva that you deserve to be. You can decide to be the selective, health-conscious actor during your trip to the grocery store and choose only organic and healthy food so as to stay svelte for your feature film shoot. You get the idea. Write your "part" below next to your daily tasks:

Daily task	How I will feel/act while doing it
_____	_____
_____	_____
_____	_____
_____	_____
_____	_____
_____	_____
_____	_____

Now, it's time to get acting. If you want, you can set alarms in your phone for five or ten minutes before your scheduled tasks for the day, reminding you to act your new part. And don't forget to don one of your success-worthy outfits from yesterday's exercise to help you look the part that you plan to embody.

DAY 4

Whether you want it to be or not, your body is part of your instrument, and whatever body you're currently in is the one you're stuck with for the foreseeable future. You've probably heard this before, but since you currently only have one of these body things, you should probably take care of it. This is particularly true because, if you're a dancer,

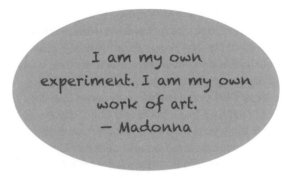

actor, or singer, or performance artist, you have to use your body to make your art. Most of us don't really grasp the difference between a body that is operating in an efficient manner and a body that is just plain operating to stay alive. The truth is, the choices you make with regard to nutrition, exercise, hydration, and sleep can make a career-changing impact on your life.

List three things you are going to do today for your health that will set yourself up for success. (And don't forget to dress for success while you do it!)

1. _____

2. _____

3. _____

DAY 5

The key to this chapter (and hopefully the rest of your life) is to set up good habits that will prepare you for a prosperous future. How do you make a habit be a habit? If you google "how to create a habit," you can find a plethora of articles on how to change your current routines and trajectory. Charles Duhigg also has a popular book about it. The long and the short of it, though, is that you can't start a new habit unless you decide what to do and when to do it. That seems like a given, but we all know somebody who has been "writing a book" for years but has never put pen to paper. Why? Probably because that person didn't schedule any writing sessions. Today you'll make plans for next week to dress and act your future part. Write two ways that you will dress the part and two ways that you will act the part and when you will do them.

Dressing the Part

1. _____

   When I will do this: _____

2. _____

   When I will do this: _____

Acting the Part

1. _____

   When I will do this: _____

2. _____

   When I will do this: _____

Ideally, you should make a plan to continue these practices for the rest of your life/career. Remember from last chapter that it takes sixty-six days to create a habit, so you could potentially start something new every three months and get it to stick. So, for instance, after dressing like a successful Broadway dancer for three months, it will hopefully become a habit for you to dress like a successful Broadway dancer; and after that becomes a habit, you will become more confident in your dance abilities in auditions; and before you know it, you'll be kicking your face on the Great White Way. Worst-case scenario? You challenge yourself to be confident, purposeful, and stylin' for a little while, and you don't succeed in your career. Hopefully, it was fun while you were trying it.

LET ME TELL YOU A STORY. . . .

Here is a cautionary tale. One day many years ago, I received a callback for a recurring featured dancer role on a network television show. I was thrilled. My friend was choreographing the television show (yay, networking for a network!) and I was excited about the prospect of my first series regular role on television. The callback happened to be February 15—the morning after Valentine's Day. On the evening of Valentine's Day, I went out with my husband to the fancy dinner that we had already planned, had a seven-course dinner with wine pairings, and then received a text from a friend to join him at an exclusive party in Soho. We went. Sometime around 3 a.m., I remembered that I had a 10 a.m. callback and that it meant a lot to me. After trudging back to our apartment in Weehawken, New Jersey, I got about four hours of sleep before the morning of the callback, and I woke up feeling terrible and guilty. Needless to say, my audition was *terrible*. It was one of those all-day callbacks for dancers, and by around 2 p.m., my vision started to get blurry and I couldn't spot or stand on one leg to save my life. My friend the choreographer didn't cut me (because he was being nice but not because I was any kind of a good dancer at that point), but when it came time to choose the dancers to appear on the show, I was (obviously) not one of their favorites. This was *ten years ago*, and I still think of that television show when I think of Valentine's Day.

The moral of this cautionary tale is: *don't give yourself a reason to have regrets*! There are *so* many things in the world of the performing arts that you can't control. The thing you *can* easily control is how you care for your physical self. Incidentally, your brain is a part of your physical self, so when you are hungry, sleepy, or dehydrated, you don't even think as quickly. Did you know that, according to a recent scientific study, dehydration "impairs cognitive performance, particularly for tasks involving attention, executive function, and motor coordination when water deficits exceed 2% BML [body mass loss]"?[3] Hydration is something you can control (and it's free!). Why would you risk impairing your performance, attention, and coordination when you can just drink more water?

Focus on caring for your instrument. Drink a lot of water, eat healthy food, try to get eight hours of sleep, and exercise. If you've read a mainstream magazine in the past decade, you know exactly what you should do, so make optimal health for the sake of your art your goal.

NOTES

1. Max Weigand, "The Science behind 'Fake It Till You Make It,'" *Medium*, December 6, 2017, https://medium.com/@MaxWeigand/the-science-behind-fake-it-till-you-make-it-3b6a4a59438b.

2. Brandon Vallorani, "Dressing for Success and the Achievement of Your Dreams." *Forbes*, February 16, 2018, https://www.forbes.com/sites/forbesbooksauthors/2018/02/16/dressing-for-success-and-the-achievement-of-your-dreams/#7f397d6c485b.

3. Matthew T. Wittbrodt and Melinda Millard-Stafford, "Dehydration Impairs Cognitive Performance," *Medicine & Science in Sports & Exercise* 50, no. 11 (November 2018): 2360–68, https://doi.org/10.1249/mss.0000000000001682.

Chapter Thirteen

Worst-Case Scenario

No, this is not the negativity chapter. Quite the opposite, in fact. This week, you'll spend some time journaling about the worst things that could happen in your future career and what you would do to pivot (turn) your way out of them. Many performers have the mentality that if they don't "make it" in exactly the career they want at exactly the right time, they're a failure altogether. That couldn't be further from the truth. Steven Spielberg didn't get in to USC's film school, J. K. Rowling was a broke and divorced single mom when she started writing the Harry Potter series, and Oprah was fired from her first TV anchor job. Everybody who is anybody has experienced failure (and if they haven't, they will). It's what we do with our failures that is the most important thing we will ever choose to do. And if one thing doesn't work out, you can switch things up to pursue something similar.

Let's say that all you've ever wanted to do in the world is nab a series regular role on a crime drama on CBS. Your chance arrived, you got the big audition, and then you didn't get a call from your agent. Don't worry; all is not lost. You could look for another television show to audition for in the near future. Or you could open up your mind to other options. Maybe you consider auditioning for a soap opera, or perhaps you open up your options to include a show on Facebook. Or perhaps you'd be a great writer of a crime drama while you're waiting on your break to act in one. You'd be surprised: most of the time the worst thing you can think of isn't too bad after all. And if you've already imagined all of the worst things that can happen and the unknown isn't so unknown, perceived failure becomes significantly less scary. Rather than being surprised by any setbacks, if you plan for what you will do when things go sideways, you will be a huge leap (grand jeté) ahead of the pack.

> Challenges are gifts that force us to search for a new center of gravity. Don't fight them. Just find a new way to stand.
> — Oprah Winfrey

LET ME TELL YOU A STORY. . . .

I believe I have said this before, but I will reiterate the fact that I was not the best bal-let dancer in the world. I was a decent ballet dancer in spite of the unfortunate genetic hand that I had been dealt, but I was never going to be a principal dancer with the New York City Ballet unless I got my feet broken and my hips replaced. Nevertheless, my whole life had revolved around ballet and the pursuit of it since I was about ten years old. When I was dancing in the corps de ballet of my third ballet company (the now defunct Lexington Ballet, in Kentucky), I was called into the artistic director's office for a talk. It turns out that I was "not suited" for the repertoire that the company had on the horizon, and I would be let go from the company after we closed our current show. I asked why, and the director talked in circles for a bit. Finally, he came out with, "You're just too big for a classical season." Keep in mind that, at this point, I was 5'6" and 120 pounds. I offered to lose weight and was met with the response, "It won't make a difference." I sighed. My pear shape had finally caught up with me, and I would be unemployed in a few weeks. I walked out of the office to gather my thoughts.

News flash: finding a job in a ballet company is not easy. Many companies do not have centralized auditions, and some companies only have openings every few years. If you are interested in auditioning for a ballet company, you should plan to drive/fly to the city in which the company rehearses for an audition or plan to send in a video. I started planning to drive around the country and audition anywhere that would have me. And boy, did I audition. After my sixth city and sixth company class (each time with a different ballet company), I was offered an apprentice position with the New Jersey Ballet. It did not pay a living wage, I would have to move to an expensive area of an expensive state, and most of the dancers preferred speaking Russian rather than English. I took the job and began to consider a life pivot. While I was learning *Cop-pelia* with the New Jersey Ballet, I began researching musical theater jobs and voice lessons. A few short years later, I was happily dancing on Broadway, never to be told to lose weight again.

When I was let go from Lexington Ballet, I was devastated. It truly seemed to me that it was the worst possible thing that could happen. If it hadn't happened, though, I would never have moved to New Jersey, I would never have auditioned for a musical in New York, and I would have missed out on more than ten years dancing and singing eight shows per week on and off Broadway. The moral of the story is that, no matter what happens, you can always alter your course and keep on truckin'.

DAY 1

Let's take a trip to the dark side. Today you'll spend some time brainstorming all of the terrible things that could happen in your career. Set a timer and imagine what would be the equivalent of your artistic apocalypse. Be brave enough to part the curtains of your worst nightmare and peer inside. Often, when we take a close look at what we think is the most dreadful outcome we can imagine, the close-up is not as scary as we thought. Perhaps you're a dancer and your worst nightmare is breaking your leg. Or maybe you're a singer who is terrified of nodes. Maybe you have other fears like bankruptcy, losing a loved one, or being alone. All of these fears are just as valid as the next one. But they are of no use to you until you get them all out in the open. So, set a timer for fifteen to twenty minutes and list all of the awful things that could happen on your trajectory to success.

_____

_____

_____

_____

_____

_____

_____

_____

_____

_____

_____

_____

_____

_____

_____

_____

_____

DAY 2

Now that you've imagined the worst, you'll think about what you'll do if the worst happens. Short of a scenario in which you perish, you will almost always have the choice to take some kind of action after the worst-case scenario takes place. If you break your leg, what will you do? Watch Netflix until it heals? Start a support group for busted dancers? Write a book? Choreograph on your friends? How about if you're a singer who finds out your tour is canceled? What will you do then? Start auditioning for new ones? Change plans? Use your saved tour money to buy an orchid farm in Hawaii and become a recluse? There is no wrong answer here. Just write the first thing that comes to your mind. Choose eight of the scariest scenarios from day 1 and really think about what you would do in that situation. We will think of this in a traditional if/then format, so put on your thinking cap.

1. If _____
   _____ happens,
   then I will _____
   _____ .

2. If _____
   _____ happens,
   then I will _____
   _____ .

3. If _____
   _____ happens,
   then I will _____
   _____ .

4. If _____
   _____ happens,
   then I will _____
   _____ .

5. If _____
   _____ happens,
   then I will _____
   _____ .

6. If _____
   _____ happens,

then I will _____

_____.

7. If _____

_____ happens,

then I will _____

_____.

8. If _____

_____ happens,

then I will _____

_____.

DAY 3

You've survived the worst-case scenario situation at least long enough to make one decision. (Well, actually, you've survived eight worst-case scenarios.) Now let's play out these ideas to see what would happen in your career *after* your first "then" decision. Just use your imagination, as you could never know what would actually happen in life. How would you choose your next moves after disaster strikes? If there's a fire that destroys all of the music in your home that you've ever written and your first move is to get out of the house and to safety, what would you do then? Call your family, move in with your sister, and start writing again? Would you write a musical about the fire? Would you find a way to retrieve some of your work? Really ask yourself, as you did in chapter 2 when you explored your *why*, and be honest. Maybe you choose to scrap writing altogether after your imaginary fire and take up teaching English as a second language. Okay. That's great. There are no wrong choices. Choose two of your favorite (or least-favorite?) scenarios from day 2 and follow the "choose your own adventure" a few more pages into the book. For each scenario, write your first "then" statement as the second "if" statement and then make a second "then" decision. Write your second decision as the third "if" statement, and so on.

Success is to be measured not so much by the position that one has reached in life as by the obstacles which he has overcome.
— Booker T. Washington

Scenario #1

If _____

_____ happens,

then I will _____.

If _____

_____ happens,

then I will _____.

If _____

_____ happens,

then I will _____.

If _____

_____ happens,

then I will _____ .

If _____

_____ happens,

then I will _____ .

Scenario #2

If _____

_____ happens,

then I will _____ .

If _____

_____ happens,

then I will _____ .

If _____

_____ happens,

then I will _____ .

If _____

_____ happens,

then I will _____ .

If _____

_____ happens,

then I will _____ .

The point of this exercise is: *You will survive and find a way to flourish one way or another.* And after this exercise, hopefully, you will be less afraid of bad things happening if you know that you will survive and that you will find a way to pivot your choices to bring yourself back to a happy place.

DAY 4

It's phone-a-friend day! Today your challenge is to reach out to a couple of friends and ask them if they have ever had anything bad happen to them. If so, ask them to tell you something good that came out of that rotten event. With hindsight, most people can look back on something seemingly all bad and find a little nugget of something good. If you don't have any friends who have had anything negative happen to them, first, you should find some friends who are a little more truthful, but second, you're more than welcome to put a post on social media inviting stories from your friends and acquaintances near and far. That's a little bit of a Pandora's box, but it will make you realize that negative experiences are a necessary part of life. Ask two friends today how they overcame bad experiences and what they learned about them afterward.

All the adversity I've had in my life, all my troubles and obstacles, have strengthened me. . . . You may not realize it when it happens, but a kick in the teeth may be the best thing in the world for you. — Walt Disney

DAY 5

Some things seem irreversible. Some things are. But most aren't. If, for instance, you have a series regular audition for *Grey's Anatomy* and you bomb it, you more than likely think that you will never again get an opportunity to nab that job. Chances are, though, if you live long enough, you will. If you audition for Glinda in *Wicked* for the fifth time and don't get the job, you think, "They're done with me and they'll never call me in again." You believe that until six months later when you get your sixth audition for the same role. The point is that when the unthinkable happens, you may think that all is lost and that your "once-in-a-lifetime" opportunity is gone for good. Guess what? Once-in-a-lifetime opportunities are often twice- or thrice-in-a-lifetime opportunities if you're wise and patient. Set a timer for ten to fifteen minutes and list all of the things that could go wrong in your career (and life, if you'd like) that could never go right or be rectified later. (This will hopefully be a very short list.)

_____

_____

_____

_____

_____

_____

_____

_____

_____

_____

_____

_____

_____

If you're like most people, you may not have been able to think of a lot of things for today's exercise. If you didn't, that's *great*! Almost everything is reversible! If you thought of a lot of things that can't be undone, then, while you may be a little bit of a pessimist, the good news is you're definitely creative.

Spending an extended amount of time imagining all of the bad things that could happen in the future is not the best thing to do all the time, but it's good to do every once in a while. Like a character shining a light down a dark hallway in a horror movie, looking at potential problems either makes them significantly less scary or it informs you so that you can make wise decisions to continue to thrive when bad things happen.

Chapter Fourteen

Pay It Forward

Artists can sometimes have a reputation of being, well, a little selfish. Picture the actress portrayed as the diva who spends more on sunglasses than most people earn in a month. Or the singer-songwriter who's so obsessed with perfection that he forces his team to work for twenty-four hours without a meal break. Sure, these are stereotypes, but it's surprisingly easy to get overly wrapped up in your art, your ambition, and the world you create for yourself. This can be great for your overall productivity but not so great for your humanity. Volunteering not only makes you feel good but it can also increase the perception that you have more time. According to a study cited in the *Harvard Business Review*, people who spent time helping others felt more "time affluent" than people who did other things.[1] Helping others may seem superfluous but, in fact, it is a win/win endeavor and is key to a well-rounded life.

You do not need to be megarich to donate to a charity or volunteer your time. In fact, some of the most significant things you can do for others involve offering a kind word to someone who needs encouragement or spending some of your time planting a garden or building a new structure. Again, you don't need to create a million-dollar endowment to be considered a charitable person. Small deeds can have more impact than you may even be able to see, and the more you do for others, the better you feel about yourself. You can volunteer to teach free dance classes or send a weekly letter to your great-aunt.

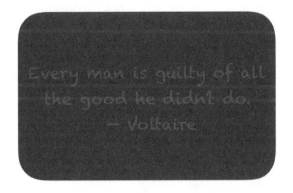

Every man is guilty of all the good he didn't do.
— Voltaire

You can buy a sandwich for the homeless lady on the corner or take meals to homebound elderly people. There are thousands of ways to make your community a better place, so you should find something that you enjoy and find rewarding.

This week you'll choose a cause that has nothing to do with your career (but one that you're passionate about) and donate your time, money, and/or resources toward

157

it—or just raise awareness for it. Your cause could be as large as curing cancer or as small as volunteering to help a friend move. Once you find a great cause to which to donate your resources, you should make a (realistic) commitment to do it on a regular basis.

LET ME TELL YOU A STORY. . . .

You meet a lot of pretty awesome people when you volunteer. I recently went to my friend Kelly Wilson's birthday party (shout out Kelly!) and met so many people. In fact, her sit-down brunch at a fancy vegan restaurant in West Hollywood was a gathering of thirty of the most beautiful and successful (and some famous) Los Angeles movers and shakers. Kelly, among other things, is a pretty great actress. But she also provides a home for rescued dogs and is an activist for a number of worthy charities. *This* is where she met most of these amazing people. Producers, influencers, agents, and even an *American Idol* finalist were in attendance at her birthday party, and it was a networker's dream. Should you volunteer to support animal rights so that you can meet famous people? No. That's weird. But adding some new contacts to your networking master list is an added bonus. And so is feeling good about the fact that you're making the world a better place.

One more story: when I was living in New York, I volunteered for a charity called Broadway Big Brother/Big Sister that paired performers with underprivileged youth to learn and perform shows together. I worked with the organizer and choreographer, Lainie, for a number of years, and I am still friends with one of my "little sisters" and many of the other grown-up performers. It was a joyous occasion that I looked forward to, and it gave me so much energy and fulfillment that I volunteered every year. It also made me aware of the types of struggles kids endured in the New York area and made me so grateful for my current situation and my comfortable and supported childhood. And, to boot, when the organizer of the event was not able to teach her regularly scheduled lucrative summer teaching gig in Sydney, Australia, she called me and offered me the opportunity to step in as her replacement. I cannot emphasize enough that paying it forward has no downside and that everyone should seek out opportunities to spend time or money to improve their communities.

DAY 1

What do you care about? No, not whether one of the *Real Housewives of Beverly Hills* will win their lawsuit. What do you *really* care about? What injustices in this world do you want to change? What is slowly going toward ruin that most people don't understand? The goal of today's brainstorm is to find one thing that you're very passionate about changing while you're on this planet. It could be climate change, pediatric cancer, autism, human trafficking, ocean pollution, animal rights, education, feeding the homeless, mental health advocacy, building playgrounds, or anything in between. Set a timer for ten to fifteen minutes and list all of the things you are passionate about improving in your community and on our planet (and even beyond!).

_____

_____

_____

_____

_____

_____

_____

_____

_____

_____

_____

_____

_____

_____

_____

_____

DAY 2

Great! You care! Now comes the hard part: choosing. Like any good parent, I'm sure that all of the babies you listed above are important to you. But for the sake of getting a good start, let's choose *one* cause from the list. You can always come back later to this list, choose a second cause, and make twice the impact.

The cause I choose to support is:

_____

Now that you have chosen your cause, it's time to do a little research. You'd be surprised how many charities, activist groups, events, and movements already exist. Take some time to search out what group you would like to work with to support your cause. Or perhaps, after you do some research, you will choose to step out on your own and start your own charity! You can't know what you want to do, though, until you know what's out there. Set a timer for ten to fifteen minutes, do some research, and list all of the groups that support your cause.

_____

_____

_____

_____

_____

_____

_____

_____

_____

_____

_____

_____

_____

_____

_____

_____

DAY 3

Look back at yesterday and choose the charity you would like to work with. (Or choose to create one of your own.)

The charity I choose to work with is: _____.

Service to others is the rent you pay for your room here on earth. — Muhammad Ali

You've got a cause and a charity. Now what are you going to do? Well, there are a multitude of ways to support a cause. You can volunteer for a charity's events, you can raise money to support their efforts, you can use your social media and your network to raise awareness for the cause, or you can create a whole new way to support their (and your!) efforts. If you chose to step out on your own to support a cause rather than joining the efforts of an already existing charity, you should ask yourself this question as well: What am I going to do? First, survey your resources and decide how you might use what you have to support your cause. Perhaps you're an avid runner; you may decide to raise money for your charity by running a marathon. Or, if you have a large following on YouTube, perhaps you choose to make a video to raise awareness for your cause. Or maybe you're passionate about youth homelessness and you're a great teacher, so you choose to volunteer to teach writing classes to homeless youth. No matter what you choose, remember that being affiliated with a charity and being passionate about a cause is pointless if you don't actually *do* something to change the world. Take ten to fifteen minutes and list the ways you could promote the charity you've chosen to create or assist:

_____

_____

_____

_____

_____

_____

_____

_____

Now, choose the one way you would like to start contributing: _____

_____

DAY 4

Do you ever wonder why so many companies have an "Invite a Friend" option that gives you a reward if you refer someone? Duh. Because two buyers or users is almost always better than one. If you're passionate about your cause, one of the best things you can do is to invite a similarly passionate friend to join you in your efforts to change the world. Inviting this extra person will help you do double the good deeds and will also give you and your friend a new shared experience and make your friendship bond even stronger. So, when choosing a friend to invite to help promote your cause, think of someone in your network with whom you would like to have a better connection. Reach out today with some ideas, and see if your friend is interested in joining your quest. If he or she says no, move on to the next friend. It's never considered a bad thing to ask a person to help out to promote a worthy cause.

Today, I will reach out to _____ to help me fight the good fight!

DAY 5

It's day 5 and it's time to make a plan. You have your cause, you have your charity, you have your event or action, and you have your buddy. The only thing left to do is to *do it*! Schedule your good deeds. If you're going to do a charity run/walk, set up your training schedule. If you are going to volunteer at a soup kitchen, call the place, set up dates that you will be there, and add those dates to your calendar. If you're going to raise awareness via your social media, set up a post schedule or video/photo shoot. Whatever it is, you must plan it to do it—and stick to it. Here is your official pay-it-forward Mad Lib:

I will do _____ for

_____ (charity or cause) on

_____ (day/time) with

_____ (your buddy). I will continue to support

this cause by doing _____ and I

will do this on _____ (regularly scheduled days/times).

Sometimes things can seem like a huge deal when they actually aren't. You fall asleep in your dressing room and miss your cue to go onstage for your big solo. Or you get cut from a dance audition in front of all of your friends. Volunteering to help out with a worthy cause can help you realize that things like getting dropped by your agent or manager are not disasters. A hurricane is a disaster. Missing your call time can seem significantly less dramatic after spending time with an elderly woman in hospice care. Or rescuing a dog. Or feeding hungry children. If you pay it forward, you can't help but also pay yourself.

NOTE

1. Cassie Mogilner, "You'll Feel Less Rushed If You Give Time Away," *Harvard Business Review*, September 27, 2017, https://hbr.org/2012/09/youll-feel-less-rushed-if-you-give-time-away.

Chapter Fifteen

Your Virtual Marquee

We have to talk about it because it's a part of our culture that is not going away any time soon: social media. If you're an aspiring artist looking for exposure in any field, social media is one of your most valuable tools. Now that you know exactly what you want to achieve, what makes you special, who can help you achieve your dreams, what you should look and act like to get the part, and you've been working toward excellence as an artist and a human . . . it's time to share all of that with the world. This week, you'll cultivate your social media plan to show yourself and your artistry to the (virtual) world.

What's the best online platform for your art? What is your social media aesthetic? Are you sweet or sarcastic? Edgy? Gritty? Conscientiously buttoned up? Grounded? While you're thinking about this kind of thing, don't forget to refer back to chapter 9 to make sure that your social media aesthetic matches your style. What established artist's social media do you admire, and what do you enjoy about it? How often will you post to your social media? These are all important questions that you probably have not considered in the past. You probably already use social media, but if you're like most of the world, you don't really think too much about the image you are putting out there. Most folks see something, take a picture of it, and post it without thinking. If you are purposeful about what you post to your platforms and how you present yourself, you might be able to nab more auditions, gain some recognition, or even get a great job.

This book is not intended to help you get to one hundred thousand followers in a month. That's a valiant goal, but that is a whole other book. Or ten books. Gaining followers in today's congested landscape is harder than it seems, but there is some great advice out there on how to cultivate your audience. Pick up a book or read articles or blogs on social media marketing if you feel that cultivating a large social media following is important to your success in your field. Right now, though, the most important thing to do in relation to your social media is to become aware of how it is reflecting you, your personality, and your work.

Think of this chapter as similar to creating your VIP list in chapter 10. It's important to keep in touch with the people on your VIP list, and it's also important to keep current on your social media. Why? So that the folks you don't even know who are on your VIP list can keep up with your artistic pursuits. You know your friends follow what you're up to, but you don't necessarily know if your mom's sister Karen's hairdresser is totally into everything you create and will be an undercover fan of yours for the rest of her life. You also never know if your mom's sister Karen's hairdresser knows anyone else in the business and could five years in the future mention you to the casting director who will book you on your dream job. Is that likely? No. There's definitely a very slim chance of this happening. But hey, if you buy enough lottery tickets for long enough, you will eventually win some dough. And social media is free marketing for you and your art. It's a win/win.

Now this may go without saying, but you should know that what you put out there on social media can be seen by *everyone* (unless you have your settings set to private). Even if your brand is the edgy bad boy, it's probably not a good idea to post photos of inebriated you partying until dawn

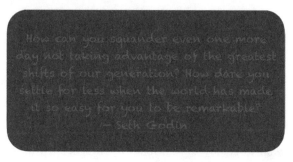

How can you squander even one more day not taking advantage of the greatest shifts of our generation? How dare you settle for less when the world has made it so easy for you to be remarkable?
— Seth Godin

for the whole world to see. You may be the most responsible person in the universe, but if producers, casting directors, or choreographers check out your Instagram feed and see these pictures, they may reconsider hiring you for their project based on their erroneous assumption that you are irresponsible. The long and short of it is that you should never give anybody any excuse not to hire you based on what you post on social media.

LET ME TELL YOU A STORY. . . .

I have seen a few auditions in Los Angeles lately that have the following written in the character breakdown: "100,000 or more followers preferred." Like any rational human being, my first reaction to that addendum to a breakdown is an exasperated eye roll. But if you think about it from a producer's standpoint, it makes sense. Let's say you are a producer who is making a low-budget indie feature film on a $50,000 budget. You will spend every dime on the creation and editing of the film, leaving you with no leftover money to spend on advertisement. So what do you do? Well, you have your cast advertise for you. If you cast a secondary role with a good actress who has hundreds of thousands of fans on social media and then you add a clause into her contract that she has to post at least five times about the film to all of her social media channels, you just got yourself some free advertising. What if there are two actresses you want for the same part, and one has 4,000 followers and the other has 1.4 million? Guess who is most likely to be cast if all other things are equal? You guessed it.

This is not the way that every film, show, commercial, and other project works by any stretch of the imagination. I highly doubt that CBS takes the time to look to see if someone has a huge social media following when they're casting a costar on

Young Sheldon. Smaller projects, though, are a different story. "But the best actor/ dancer/singer should always get the part, not the one who has the most followers! It's not fair!" you might say. I hear you. And to some extent, I agree. But we all learned in grade school that life often isn't fair. Sometimes the best person for the part gets the part. Most often, though, there are many other factors besides talent that go into casting. If you can create a large and distinct enough virtual presence for yourself, you can increase your chances of being cast, your likelihood of receiving funding for projects, and your ability to rustle up other opportunities for your career. Again, the more people who know about you and what you do, the better.

Incidentally, we all instinctually know that there is a fine line we all need to walk on social media between self-promotion and humanness. The "humble brag" reigns supreme these days, and it can leave folks with a taste in their mouth worse than orange juice after toothpaste. "My phone was hacked and I just texted something in Japanese to Taylor Swift *and* Zendaya. I'm so embarrassed!" (insert eye roll here). Whatever your platform, you should decide how you are going to approach your viewers, and it definitely shouldn't be like the previous statement. Once you decide what your approach is, as long as you stay true to it and completely transparent, you're golden. Take, for instance, Nordstrom. I know that a Nordstrom ad is going to come up on my Instagram on a regular basis (usually showing me a deal on a new pair of pumps—they know me well). I'm not annoyed by this, because I have already assumed that Nordstrom is going to try to sell me things. That's what they do. And they usually have figured out what I want to buy from my search history, so they're essentially adding value to my life by decreasing the amount of time I need to spend looking for leopard-print, four-inch-stiletto, thigh-high suede boots. If, however, someone who has not been in touch in a while suddenly reaches out to try to sell me some new pyramid-scheme item without first asking how I am, I get a little grumpy. Why? Because my acquaintance has crossed the unwritten rules of engagement and has stepped outside my expectations of an appropriate contact. So, if your Instagram is promotional for, say, your choreography, stay true to that. Don't suddenly start posting a lot of random family photos because those who are interested in choreography (and not your grandma Joanie) will probably choose to stop following you. If you give people what they know they will be getting from you, they will continue to engage.

Now, the term "friend" is a little loose. People mock the "friending" on social media, and say, "Gosh, no one could have 300 friends!" Well, there are all kinds of friends. Those kinds of "friends," and work friends, and childhood friends, and dear friends, and neighborhood friends, and we-walk-our-dogs-at-the-same-time friends, etc. — Gretchen Rubin

DAY 1

It's time for some research—social media style. Today, you'll spend some time perusing social media (like you don't do that every day) to find artists who are pursuing careers in your field. Look at what they're putting out there and how they're presenting it. Take notes on what you would like to incorporate into your online presence and what you don't think will work for you. Check out multiple platforms to see which has the most engagement in your field. Do screenwriters tend to gather around the Twitter water cooler? Do most dancers post videos on Instagram rather than Pinterest or Facebook? What seems to be the demographic of each platform, and how does it match up to your target audience for your artistic pursuits? The goal of all of this information gathering is to find how you want to represent yourself. But first, we just want to gather information on what you like and don't like and whether you think specific tactics or aesthetics work or not. Here is an example of some research from an aspiring comedic actor:

Person or group: Tituss Burgess
Social Platform: Instagram
What I like/don't like: I like that he posts hilarious videos but that they're always in his character's voice.
How I can apply that to my social presence: I have a lot of characters I embody in my work, but I can create a series of videos featuring all of my favorite characters.

Set a timer for fifteen to twenty minutes, seek out similar artists' social media, record what you like and don't like, and decide how you can incorporate what you like (or keep out what you don't like) into your own digital materials.

Person or group: _____

Social Platform: _____

What I like/don't like: _____

How I can apply that to my social presence: _____

_____

_____

Person or group: _____

Social Platform: _____

What I like/don't like: _____

How I can apply that to my social presence: _____

_____

_____

Person or group: _____

Social Platform: _____

What I like/don't like: _____

How I can apply that to my social presence: _____

_____

_____

Person or group: _____

Social Platform: _____

What I like/don't like: _____

How I can apply that to my social presence: _____

_____

_____

Person or group: _____

Social Platform: _____

What I like/don't like: _____

How I can apply that to my social presence: _____

_____

_____

Person or group: _____

Social Platform: _____

What I like/don't like: _____

How I can apply that to my social presence: _____

_____

_____

Person or group: _____

Social Platform: _____

What I like/don't like: _____

How I can apply that to my social presence: _____

_____

_____

Person or group: _____

Social Platform: _____

What I like/don't like: _____

How I can apply that to my social presence: _____

_____

_____

DAY 2

Now we will spend some time deciding what you want your social media presence to look/feel/sound like and where you want to focus most of your energy. Choose two main social media platforms on which to focus your presence and decide what your niche will be on them. This should tie back to chapter 9 and fit in with your understanding of your artistic style. You should also take into consideration the things you identified that make you stand out from the crowd from chapter 7. Finally, you should always hearken back to chapter 2 and your *me* words. These should all feel like they're in the same family . . . because they are: the family of the entity that is *you*! Let's make some decisions. Don't worry: any decision you make can be undone and/or pivoted in the future if it doesn't work out.

My ME words are:

_____

_____

_____

A few things that make me different are:

_____

_____

_____

My artistic style is:

_____

_____

Review:

My Social Media Specifics:

My main social media platform will be: _____

My secondary social media platform will be (if any): _____

The purpose of my Internet presence is to: _____

_____

_____

Three ways you will know it's my "voice" (e.g., "It's sarcastic" or "It has bright colors"):

_____

_____

_____

_____

DAY 3

Can you post photos, witty comments, videos, and other content whenever you encounter or create it? Sure, but it's not efficient. And remember that your goal is to support your artistry, so the more efficient and thoughtful you can be about your social accounts, the better. Today you will start gathering and planning to create the content that you will put out into the world. Create a folder on the desktop of your personal computer and title it "Social Content." This is where you will place all of the things you plan to share with the world before you share it. Go through all of your old photos, recordings (audio and video), pieces you've written in the past, or anything you haven't shared with the world that you would like to share. Place it into this folder and as you share it, take it out. This way, you will always have a place to put content and you will always know what you have already shared.

Next, you'll decide how and when you will create new content. If you're a dancer, perhaps you'll set up time to go into a dance studio with a friend and film some brilliant videos (or maybe you'll choose a different and fun alternative location, like an old warehouse or your local pool). Or if you've decided that photos are your thing, set up an informal shoot. If you're a singer, buy a buddy dinner in exchange for attending your next cabaret performance to film your vocal prowess. You should plan to create whatever you decide is the thing you'll be putting out there into the world.

So set up a time to capture content that matches the vision you created yesterday. If you have decided that your tone is dark and introspective, you should probably not plan to go do a photo shoot on the beach. You get the idea. Take a moment to plan, and then schedule your first content creation appointment. It could be an appointment with yourself to write a regularly occurring blog, an appointment with a friend to film some kooky improv scenes, or a session with a professional photographer. Artist's choice.

One type of content I plan to create is: _____

I will create this content (circle one)   Daily   Weekly   Monthly   Other_____

Scheduled date/time for next content creation session: _____

Reminder: put it in your planner or calendar, and keep the appointment!

LET ME TELL YOU A STORY. . . .

My friend Tabitha Blue has a really beautiful blog and social media presence called Fresh Mommy Blog. I always know that I will be inspired by her gorgeous photos, the grateful and welcoming tone of her comments, and her multitude of adorable children. She takes the time to set up shoots that show her beautiful family and DIY home adventures so that she can use that material for future posts. She does *not* carry her super fancy camera around with her every moment of every day and stop the progress of her life to document it. Why? This would encroach upon what she is actually aiming to do: be a really great mommy. The moral of the story is that the main thing should stay the main thing when it comes to social media. Chances are, social media is not your main thing, so while it is definitely something to pay attention to, do not let it take time away from pursuing your art.

DAY 4

Let's talk a little about frequency when it comes to social media. You all know that we need to be selective about how much content we put out there. Well, we don't *have* to. But either way, you should make a conscious decision about your social media posting frequency. If you're purposeful about when you share things, there is a chance that people will come to look forward to hearing from/seeing/reading about you. For me, Wednesdays are one of my favorite weekdays because I know that on Wednesday evenings after my son goes to bed, I will be partaking in my favorite guilty pleasure—watching *Survivor* on CBS. I would probably still watch *Survivor* if it came on at varying times during the week, but there is something special about anticipating watching it on a schedule.

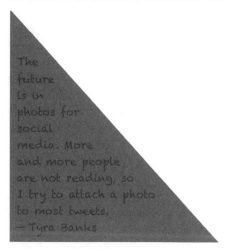

The future is in photos for social media. More and more people are not reading, so I try to attach a photo to most tweets.
— Tyra Banks

Even if you don't expect people to wait with bated breath for your next YouTube video, it can't hurt to decide when you will post content to the Internet. Everything you can plan in advance takes away brainpower for other more important decisions in the future. If you know exactly when you will put out new content, you don't have to worry about whether you've posted too much or if you've lost everyone's attention. One decision on the frequency of your content release eliminates a plethora of decisions in the future and frees up your time and brain space for other more important decisions. (Incidentally, this is why some people say Steve Jobs always wore a black turtleneck, that he wanted to save his decision-making power for more important things than what he wore.) So let's decide when you're going to release your content into the world.

One more thing: it's okay if the start date for your social media plan is not today. Perhaps you need more time to create content or you want to get all of your ducks in a row before you quack loudly across the worldwide pond. Make some frequency decisions in relation to your future social media engagement below:

Frequency with which I will release content to my main social media platform:

_____

_____

Frequency with which I will release content to my secondary social media platform (if any): _____

_____

I will begin releasing this brilliant onslaught of artistic wonderfulness to the world on (date): _____

_____

Now put these into your calendar as recurring appointments and keep them! Go!

DAY 5

The last thing you should consider is using your friends to create a SMOD—your own personal social media pod (no, that's not a real acronym). Creating pods is a way groups can get together and encourage engagement in each other's content. While there are huge groups of folks that have thousands of members, the best way to get a SMOD started is to grab a group of your besties and make a pact to like and comment on things that each of you contribute to the world at large. Because, at the time of this publication, some social media algorithms push the posts with the most engagement to the top of feeds, the more folks who engage with your stuff, the more likely more people will be to see it. It doesn't take a lot of time, and it can't hurt to keep up to date with what your friends are up to as well. List your top ten supporters below: those who you believe will be interested in banding together to get the word out about each other's stuff. Then reach out to the people on your list and set up some guidelines for supporting each other online.

People I would like to invite to support each other's social media presence:

1. _____
2. _____
3. _____
4. _____
5. _____
6. _____
7. _____
8. _____
9. _____
10. _____

Proposed guidelines for my social media pod (e.g., We will reshare each other's content at least once per month, or we will like all of each other's content when it is posted):

_____

_____

_____

_____

_____

Reach out to your most willing friends and get the conversation started!

Chapter Sixteen

Curtain Call

By spending the past fifteen weeks working toward stepping into your future career in a purposeful and conscious way, you have done yourself a huge service. A lot of artists do not consider the business side of their art and, even more important, don't intentionally plan for what they want and how to get it. In short, you are already one step ahead of most artists. Regret is a potent emotion because it is sourced in the past. News flash: you can't change the past. Do not be the person who chooses an easier path only to look back ten years from now and regret not giving it your all. You should make every effort to craft the life that you want and the career that you will love.

Now the question is, How do you work all of the information from all of the exercises in this book into your already overly scheduled life? You don't want to, for instance, set up your VIP list and not continue to add to it. You also don't want to stop researching new opportunities or examining and reimagining your style. This chapter will give you a monthly plan for keeping up with every aspect of your career. This may be too "scheduled" for you, and you might want to do your own thing. You do you, boo. I encourage you to create the path that works best for your life. For those of us who prefer to be told what to do rather than thinking it up ourselves, this is our chapter.

WEEK 1

One thing you will always do is work on your art. Remember from chapter 11, though, that the best practice is focused practice. This is something you should do every day for the rest of your life (with some breaks). If you are passionate about your artistry, this should seem less like a chore than a joy. Sometimes

> Start where you are. Use what you have. Do what you can.
> — Arthur Ashe

it's hard to get started, but once you are doing what you love to do best, you should be in your element. If you are not, then perhaps you should consider a different life path; you can always sing, dance, act, or create art as a hobby. If you have chosen to go full throttle toward a career in the arts, then before you do anything, you should decide when and how you will be honing your skills and furthering your artistic journey. Schedule your practice time for this week and decide what you will be focusing on. You could invite a friend to join you, you could work on your memorization skills, or you could challenge yourself to create original content. Artist's choice. But it must be a purposeful choice. List how and when you will work on your art below.

Monday

What I will work on: _____

I will work on it from: _____ to _____

Tuesday

What I will work on: _____

I will work on it from: _____ to _____

Wednesday

What I will work on: _____

I will work on it from: _____ to _____

Thursday

What I will work on: _____

I will work on it from: _____ to _____

Friday

What I will work on: _____

I will work on it from: _____ to _____

    Now that you have decided when and how you will be practicing, let's discuss what other aspects of your career you'll be focusing on this week.

Monday

No matter how old and successful you may become, it will never hurt to continue to brainstorm new potential gigs for your art and your side hustle. The industry changes quickly, and, as you continue to learn more about the business, new potential opportunities will arise that you didn't even know could be opportunities. So, on the first Monday of every month, you should consider reopening your mind to other possibilities. Set a timer for fifteen to twenty minutes and brainstorm all of the exciting things you could do with your career and how to make some dough outside your career.

    When you're done with this brainstorm, reiterate your three main ideal gigs that you want to focus on for the next month and write them down in a place that you see every day.

Tuesday

It's research day. No matter how long you are in an industry, you can always learn more about it. Why? Things change every day. When you look at the arts, you see that audience preference changes, mediums change, and the power players involved regularly shift. You can never do too much research. Search for what is popular, who is currently doing great work, and find people in your industry who are doing what you want to be doing. Remember to search the web, talk to your friends, and even reach out to people you don't yet know. Divide your time today in half and spend the first half of your time researching.

    For the second half of your time on this lovely Tuesday, you will either connect with or add one person to your VIP list. Hopefully you have been adding to your list since you started it in chapter 10, but if you haven't, this is your opportunity to get started. First, choose whether you want to reach out and send a message to someone you already have on your list or you want to try to connect with and add a new person to your contacts. Then do some research if necessary and reach out after that. Don't forget to add your contact date, method, and message to your nifty spreadsheet so you can reference it for the future.

Wednesday

It is declared that Wednesday shall henceforth be known as "money day," and all artists throughout the land shall tally their shillings to prepare for the arrival of winter days. (Somewhere a herald trumpet sounds in the distance.) In all honesty, it is very important to keep an eye on your finances. Not only do you want to keep the lights on and buy groceries, but you also don't want to miss out on opportunities when they arise because you either can't afford them or have to work your side hustle. Wednesdays are the day to check in on your finances. Reevaluate what you are bringing in and how it relates to your expenses, check in to see if you're able to save more dough by spending less or earning more,

and research what current rates are for gigs in your field. You can use the Coin Calculator or create your own way to keep track of spending and income, but you must keep track in order to know how to maintain or improve your current situation. Look back at day 1 of chapter 6 and reevaluate these categories on a regular, monthly basis.

Thursday

It's pay it forward day! You may have already chosen your cause and your charity in chapter 14, or you may decide to choose a different or additional one. Or you may choose to do something kind for a person who may need some love or attention this week. Send an encouraging note, volunteer to serve food to the homeless, foster a puppy, or let a friend crash on your couch. Whatever you choose, today you can either plan for your act of kindness or spend your time doing it. Remember that sometimes a small gesture that takes less than five minutes for you could completely change the trajectory of another person's day or life. You are fortunate to be alive and talented, so pay the goodness forward to another human.

Friday

You have two things to do today. First, you will spend today dressing and acting the part of the successful whatever-you-want-to-be-in-the-future, and second, you will plan your social media strategy for next week. The first part is fun and easy. Look at your plans for your Friday and decide how you can present and be the best version of yourself in all of your endeavors. Look back at chapter 12 if you need any inspiration or ideas on how to get started. And don't forget to act the part of the successful and gracious artist as well.

For the second part, planning your social media for the week, decide when you will post what. If something comes up during the week that you want to address on your social, you can always add to your planned posts, but what a great way to take some stress off your weekly plate if you already know what and when you will be engaging. You can even automate these posts if you want (there are tons of apps for that) and take one more thing off your brain for the coming week. Remember to take into account the style that you cultivated in chapter 9 and to make sure that you are representing yourself in the most authentic way you can.

WEEK 2

Before you do anything else, decide when and how you will improve your artistic prowess this week. Purposeful practice makes prosperous professionals. You don't *always* have to want to start doing what you do best, but you should like doing it most of the time.

Monday

What I will work on: _____

I will work on it from: _____ to _____

Tuesday

What I will work on: _____

I will work on it from: _____ to _____

Wednesday

What I will work on: _____

I will work on it from: _____ to _____

Thursday

What I will work on: _____

I will work on it from: _____ to _____

Friday

What I will work on: _____

I will work on it from: _____ to _____

Monday

If you're not in over your head, how do you know how tall you are? — T. S. Eliot

The goal is to become a working professional artist who supports a comfortable lifestyle with money made from doing what you love. Until then, though, most people will have to get their side hustle on. So you should dedicate today to all things side hustle. Either you need to do some research to find a new side hustle or you have a great one that you can expand upon. Are you a personal trainer? Spend today advertising for new clients. Lyft driver? Set your driving schedule for the next month. Do you make jewelry to sell? Sign up for a booth at your local holiday bazaar. Remember that you're aiming for maximum money with mega flexibility.

Tuesday

It's research and VIP list day. "But wait," you might say, "we did this last week." Yes. We did do research and work on your VIP list last week. And we will do it again today . . . and next Tuesday . . . and hopefully every Tuesday for the rest of our lives. Because knowing as much as possible about your industry and making genuine contacts in your community are paramount to your success. Choose a topic to research today and dive deep. What is touring Europe as a dancer with a music artist like? Ask a friend to connect you with someone who is currently on tour, to ask questions. Or spend some time watching the Instagram stories of dancers on tour. Your research does not need to be super formal, and it should also be fun. After you do some research, trick out your VIP list. Make a new contact, reach out to someone you have not kept in touch with recently, or ask a friend to suggest some folks you should meet. People don't succeed on their own in any field and, as long as you remain the kind and generous person you are, you can only benefit from meeting and cultivating relationships with new people, so get to networking.

Wednesday

It's money day again. This Wednesday, you will choose a long-term financial goal and work backward to find how you can save up or prepare for it. Dream big. Do you want to buy a Ferrari in ten years? Buy a house? Save a lot of money? You can do anything with time and patience. Look back at day 5 of chapter 6 if you need a little more instruction on doing this exercise. You'll also want to check in today on your day-to-day finances. If you're the type of person who does not like to look at your checking account, today is the day to take a peek and make sure everything is still in order. And if it's not, don't forget to make a plan to fix it as soon as possible.

Thursday

What's the worst that could happen? This question is pretty commonplace, but many people don't actually explore the answer. You guessed it: today is worst-case-scenario day. Choose one terrible event that could happen in your life or career and then decide how you would pivot to continue to thrive even after facing adversity. Don't be afraid to get into thinking about the small details, and always take the time write it all down. The more you do this exercise, the more you will realize that you can overcome almost anything. And the more you realize that you can overcome anything, the braver you will become.

Friday

If people judge books by their covers, today is the day to bedazzle your "cover." Much like last Friday, you should spend today dressing and acting the part of the successful artist that you hope to become. Perhaps you spend today working on expanding your wardrobe or getting a new haircut. Watch YouTube and try new makeup tactics or plan your next week of workouts. You can choose hundreds of affordable things to do to make you stand out when you enter a room. While you're tricking out your look, revisit your social media plan for next week and perhaps create or plan to create new content to post for your adoring fans.

WEEK 3

Any small thing that you consistently do will make a large impact. As you continue to climb the mountain of artistic accomplishment, remember that most people are not planning and executing purposeful practice on a regular basis. You are slowly but surely distancing yourself from the pack with each day that you decide how and

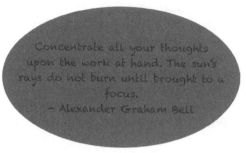

Concentrate all your thoughts upon the work at hand. The sun's rays do not burn until brought to a focus.
— Alexander Graham Bell

when you will improve your skills and your artistry. Don't forget that you can invite a friend to join you to give feedback, and make sure to note things you did that you liked and things that need improvement. Make your plans for this week's sessions below.

Monday

What I will work on: _____

I will work on it from: _____ to _____

Tuesday

What I will work on: _____

I will work on it from: _____ to _____

Wednesday

What I will work on: _____

I will work on it from: _____ to _____

Thursday

What I will work on: _____

I will work on it from: _____ to _____

Friday

What I will work on: _____

I will work on it from: _____ to _____

Monday

This Monday, make a point to reconnect with your mentor. Choose one or two specific things on which you would like to get some feedback, gather what you would like to share about what you are up to, and reach out. If you aren't happy with your current mentor, spend some time researching who you would like to approach to fill his or her shoes. Remember that you should be respectful, detailed, and positive. And make sure to keep up with what your mentor is doing so that you can either ask questions, send along congratulations, or tailor your communication based on what is going on in your mentor's life and career.

Tuesday

Remember that you can never be too knowledgeable about what is going on in your field, so take time today to focus on the future. Because the entertainment industry changes by the day, try digging into what is new and fresh in your industry and how you can grow your skills, your style, and your materials to keep up with the Joneses. Perhaps the newest trend is actors doing their own stunts, underwater partner dancing, or singing upside down while riding an elephant. Whatever it is, you are better for being in the know about what's new and popular and even better for potentially working to make yourself viable for crazy new trends. After you do your research, reach out to reconnect with at least one person on your VIP list, and don't forget to log your communication.

Wednesday

For today's money day, you will check in with your checking, savings, and credit card accounts to make sure you aren't paying any extra money that you didn't know about. Does your savings account have a five-dollar monthly fee that completely negates any interest you've earned? Call your bank and ask them to waive it or move your money to a bank that does not charge a fee. Do you have a recurring billing charge for that premium version of the app you purchased that you no longer use? Cancel it! Many people don't even look at their banking and credit card statements and most would be surprised to find small charges from different companies that they don't need. While a few $3.99 or so monthly charges may not seem like a lot, those charges could end up being almost $50 per month that you could be spending on something else that brings you more value. After you've reviewed charges and the like, check in on your budget and make sure you're on track. What should you do if you have gotten off track? Check in with your side hustle and see if you can work a few extra hours or pick up another client.

Thursday

It's time to take another look at your personal style as an artist. Most artists' styles change over time to accommodate the changing industry and the changing person. Most people are very different at twenty years old than they are at thirty years old, so your style and brand should shift as your personality and your goals shift. It's good to check in on a monthly basis to make sure that the materials you are putting out there in the world reflect who you are and where you want to be. Also set aside time today to check in on your website, social media accounts, résumé, and headshots to update them with any new information.

Friday

It's another Friday dress-up day. As you dress the part again today, schedule some time to do a small photo shoot for your social media. It does not need to be formal or expensive, but if you take a friend to a scenic location and make sure that you look fierce, you can get some shots to use for your social media accounts. Most smartphones have good enough cameras to get any photos you need for social media purposes. Even if you are not an artist who is onstage or in front of the camera, your adoring fans still want to see your mug from time to time. Unless you're Banksy, you will make yourself more relatable and more memorable the more you get your photo in front of people's eyeballs. So, while you're dressing the part of the successful artist, you might as well document it for the masses.

Getting an audience is hard. Sustaining an audience is hard. It demands a consistency of thought, of purpose, and of action over a long period of time. — Bruce Springsteen

WEEK 4

You guessed it. It's time to plan your practice for the week. Natural talent is nothing without practice. No person has been successful and stayed successful without hard work. In today's society, some people tend to think that artists get "discovered" and then "make it" without putting in the hours in the classroom or studio. This school of thought cannot be more false. Even if you are naturally inclined to do your art, you must hone your skills. The more you work on honing your skills, the more likely you will be to be well compensated for your work. There is no secret here. Hard work and dedicated hours will eventually yield results in any field. If you love what you do, do it often and you will eventually become an expert at it.

Monday

What I will work on: _____

I will work on it from: _____ to _____

Tuesday

What I will work on: _____

I will work on it from: _____ to _____

Wednesday

What I will work on: _____

I will work on it from: _____ to _____

Thursday

What I will work on: _____

I will work on it from: _____ to _____

Friday

What I will work on: _____

I will work on it from: _____ to _____

Monday

Start today with some brainstorming on what skill you can add to your arsenal to make you more viable in your industry. Or, if you are already working on cultivating a new skill, decide how you are going to incorporate it into your already existing tools of the trade. It could be a small thing, like a musical theater actor learning to juggle, or a more involved thing, like a dancer learning to skateboard. You could also take a marketing class or learn to design your own website. It does not have to always be a perfect complement to your craft. As long as you keep your brain in the land of the learning and continue to acquire skills, you are winning. When you decide what new skill you are going to acquire, let people know. Tell your friends and family and/or post it on your social media. Not only does this provide a little accountability, but it is also beneficial to let people know that you are continuing to learn and grow as an artist and as a human. You never know—you might just tell the right person at the right time and nab a job out of it!

Tuesday

For week 4 of Research Tuesday, find three new people that you would like to add to your VIP list and either reach out and introduce yourself or make plans to eventually meet them. Either send a direct message, plan to take a class that they're teaching, have a mutual friend introduce you, hang out by their stage door, or just write an old-fashioned letter and attach it to a not-so-old-fashioned e-mail. In order to choose your three new VIP list residents, you will probably need to do a little research. Don't forget that research does not necessarily mean reading musty books in a library or searching for things on the Internet and skimming Wikipedia. You can call, text, or e-mail friends as well, and ask those who have more experience than you for advice and information.

Wednesday

For your last money-related day of the week, if you have not already done so, find a way to set aside a small amount (or a big amount) of money to help out someone who needs it. Perhaps you choose to donate ten dollars per month to an animal rescue or you put your extra change in the cup holder of your car to give to homeless folks. Or, if you're rolling in artistic accomplishment, start your own foundation or donate a large sum to a cause you are passionate about. Big or small, the gesture of giving always improves the life of both the giver and the "givee."

Thursday

Take a trip guided by your imagination into your future perfect day. As you did in chapter 8, get as specific as you can when you are writing out the description. Where do you wake up? What do you eat? Whom do you associate with? Where do you work? What do you wear? While these seem like insignificant details, they actually are far from insignificant. The more specific you can be when you are imagining your future, the more specific you will be about how you go about pursuing it. For instance, if you envision your supportive and secure friends in the future, you might be less likely to spend time with your Negative Nelly paranoid complainer of a friend in the present. When you are imagining your perfect day, don't forget to take into consideration your *why*, your *me*, and the aspects of your personality, appearance, and talents that make you different from everyone else.

Friday

For the last Friday of the month, take a look back at what you have accomplished over the past thirty(ish) days. Congratulate yourself on the things you have done well. No, truly stop down and think of a few things that you kicked a-- on this month (because you inevitably did). You are actively taking charge of your future and making the world a better place through your art, your relationships, your gracious contributions to society, and your humanity. You should be proud, inspired, and excited. You *are* the future. And the future looks dazzling.

Epilogue

Thank you. If you are an artist, I genuinely thank you. And I thank you for taking the time to read and work through this book with the tenacity that I am confident you will apply to becoming the artist you are meant to be. Art transcends language, politics, race, and gender. It touches our souls on an emotional level that unites us as humans in a world that is often fractured. Art breaks down barriers, mends broken relationships, and inspires us to act on our passions. Those who pursue the arts as a career must be brave enough to bare their hearts and share their innermost vulnerability for all to see. This willingness to repeatedly reveal one's genuine humanity is both visceral and arduous. This willingness is also the very reason that artists unceasingly change the world. The life of an artist is not an easy one. It is a life of service, a life of sacrifice, and a life not without trials. It is also a life that brims with joy, a life that is authentically gratifying, and a calling that, if heard, should not be ignored. Friends, if you have heard this siren's call, I incite you to go forward bravely and change the world for the better.

Bibliography

Anderson, Amy Rees. "Never Say Anything about Yourself That You Don't Want to Come True." *Forbes*, January 21, 2015. https://www.forbes.com/sites/amyanderson/2015/01/20/never-say-anything-about-yourself-that-you-dont-want-to-come-true/#6b2d67136f98.

Clear, James. *Atomic Habits: An Easy and Proven Way to Build Good Habits and Break Bad Ones*. London: Random House Business Books, 2018.

Darrisaw, Michelle. "Lindsay Lohan Credits Oprah for Positively Transforming Her Life." *Oprah Magazine*, October 18, 2019. https://www.oprahmag.com/entertainment/tv-movies/a25834367/lindsay-lohan-oprah-beach-club-interview.

Davenport, Ken. "Some Startling New Statistics on Broadway Musical Adaptations vs. Original Shows." *The Producer's Perspective* (blog). May 1, 2014. https://www.theproducersperspective.com/my_weblog/2014/05/some-startling-new-statistics-on-broadway-musical-adaptations-vs-original-shows.html.

Gelman, Andrew. "The Average American Knows How Many People?" *New York Times*, February 18, 2013. https://www.nytimes.com/2013/02/19/science/the-average-american-knows-how-many-people.html.

Huddleston, Cameron. "58% Of Americans Have Less Than $1,000 in Savings, Survey Finds." Yahoo! Finance. May 15, 2019. https://finance.yahoo.com/news/58-americans-less-1-000-090000503.html.

Jorgenson, T. "6 Things We Can Learn from Olympic Athletes." Mayo Clinic. February 9, 2018. https://dahlc.mayoclinic.org/2018/02/09/6-things-we-can-learn-from-olympic-athletes.

Loeb, Walter. "Amazon Is the Biggest Investor in the Future, Spends $22.6 Billion on R&D." *Forbes*, November 6, 2018. https://www.forbes.com/sites/walterloeb/2018/11/01/amazon-is-biggest-investor-for-the-future/#4166e5971f1d.

Messer, Lesley. "Oprah Winfrey Remembers Her Mentor Maya Angelou." ABC News. May 28, 2014. https://abcnews.go.com/Entertainment/oprah-winfrey-remembers-mentor-maya-angelou/story?id=23901061.

Mochari, Ilan. "Steve Jobs's Early Advice to Mark Zuckerberg: Go East." *Inc.*, September 29, 2015. https://www.inc.com/ilan-mochari/visit-india-creativity.html.

Mogilner, Cassie. "You'll Feel Less Rushed If You Give Time Away." *Harvard Business Review*, September 27, 2017. https://hbr.org/2012/09/youll-feel-less-rushed-if-you-give-time-away.

Robinson, Ryan. "Five Ways Sales Has Changed in Recent Years (and How to Adapt)." *Forbes*, March 13, 2019. https://www.forbes.com/sites/ryanrobinson/2019/03/13/how-sales-has-changed/#d0aed253985a.

Trafton, Anne. "In the Blink of an Eye." MIT News. January 16, 2014. http://news.mit.edu/2014/in-the-blink-of-an-eye-0116.

Vallorani, Brandon. "Dressing for Success and the Achievement of Your Dreams." *Forbes*, February 16, 2018. https://www.forbes.com/sites/forbesbooksauthors/2018/02/16/dressing-for-success-and-the-achievement-of-your-dreams/#7f397d6c485b.

Weigand, Max. "The Science behind 'Fake It till You Make It.'" *Medium*. December 6, 2017. https://medium.com/@MaxWeigand/the-science-behind-fake-it-till-you-make-it-3b6a4a59438b.

Wittbrodt, Matthew T., and Melinda Millard-Stafford. "Dehydration Impairs Cognitive Performance." *Medicine & Science in Sports & Exercise* 50, no. 11 (November 2018): 2360–68. https://doi.org/10.1249/mss.0000000000001682.

Young, Jeffrey R. "How Many Times Will People Change Jobs? The Myth of the Endlessly-Job-Hopping Millennial." EdSurge. February 19, 2019. https://www.edsurge.com/news/2017-07-20-how-many-times-will-people-change-jobs-the-myth-of-the-endlessly-job-hopping-millennial.

About the Author

Michelle Loucadoux has performed in five Broadway musicals including playing Hope Harcourt with Sutton Foster and Joel Grey in the Tony Award–winning *Anything Goes*, originating the Broadway cast of *The Little Mermaid* as Adella and eventually playing the title role of Ariel, performing the role of Babette in *Beauty and the Beast*, originating the Broadway cast of *Mary Poppins*, and singing alongside Paul McCartney in *Chance and Chemistry*. Previous to joining Broadway, she danced professionally for New Jersey Ballet, Greensboro Ballet, and Lexington Ballet; she was also a trainee at the Richmond Ballet, performing roles from the Sugar Plum Fairy in the *Nutcracker* to Balanchine's *Serenade*. She studied dance at the American Ballet Theatre School in New York and holds a bachelor of arts degree in English from Virginia Commonwealth University and a master of business administration degree from Western Governors University.

On-screen, Michelle starred in the films *Across the Universe*, *The Bounce Back*, *Still Waiting in the Wings, Subtext,* and *Unfallen* and has appeared on television in *Criminal Minds*, *Late Night with Jimmy Fallon*, and *The View*. She currently serves as the associate dean of undergraduate studies at Studio School in Los Angeles and enjoys running and reality television. She coauthored (with Shelli Margheritis) and self-published *Making It Werk: A Dancer's Guide to the Business of Dance* in 2017 and made a small human named Carter in 2018.